The Encyclopedia of
North American Indians

Volume II

Beadwork and Beadworkers–*Cherokee Phoenix*

General Editor
D. L. Birchfield

Marshall Cavendish
New York • London • Toronto

Published in 1997 by
Marshall Cavendish Corporation
99 White Plains Road
Tarrytown, NY 10591-9001
U.S.A.

Project director: Mark J. Sachner
General editor: D. L. Birchfield
Art director: Sabine Beaupré
Photo researcher: Diane Laska
Editors: Elizabeth Kaplan, MaryLee Knowlton, Judith Plumb, Carolyn Kott Washburne, Valerie J. Weber

Consulting editors: Donna Beckstrom, Jack D. Forbes, Annette Reed Crum, John Bierhorst

Picture credits: © B. & C. Alexander: 153, 154, 240, 244; © Imma Jeanne Alexander: 281; © Archive Photos: 173, 184, 185, 193, 236, 256; © Archive Photos/American Stock: 232; Courtesy of Marilou Awiakta: 282; Sabine Beaupré 1996: 162; Courtesy of Kimberly M. Blaeser: 181; © Kit Breen: 273, 275; Courtesy of Joseph Bruchac: 203; © John Burgess, The Press Democrat: 163; Courtesy of Barney Bush: 214; © Cahokia Mounds State Historic Site: 222; Courtesy of Cherokee Nation of Oklahoma: 277; © Corbis-Bettmann: 161, 164, 165, 169, 171, 180, 183, 189, 196, 205, 206, 208, 218, 268, 278; © Tee Corinne: 194; © Eugene Fisher: 247, 248, 249; © William B. Folsom 1989: 276; Courtesy of Raven Hail: 283; © 1993 Charles Hammond: 213; © John W. Herbst: 174, 176; © Robert Holmes: 229; © Richard Hunt: 251, 253, 254, 263, 264, 265, 266; © 1994 Millie Knapp: 235; © Dan Marshall Photography: 286; Courtesy of Archie Mouse, Colcord, OK: 288; © Tom Myers Photography 1995: 149, 150, 151, 199, 200, 224, 225, 226, 228; Courtesy of Panhandle-Plains Historical Museum, Research Center, Canyon, Texas: 179; The Philbrook Museum of Art, Tulsa, Oklahoma: 145; © Elaine Querry: Cover; © Reuters/Corbis-Bettmann: 239; © Susan Silberberg: 270, 271; © Elliott Smith: 261; © Richard Strauss, Smithsonian Institution: 287; © Stephen Trimble: 258, 262; © UPI/Corbis-Bettmann: 155, 156, 158, 186, 187, 211, 238, 274, 285; © Western History Collections, University of Oklahoma Library: 219, 220; © 1993 S. Kay Young: 160; © 1992 Jim Yuskavitch: 259

Library of Congress Cataloging-in-Publication Data

The encyclopedia of North American Indians.
     p. cm.
     Includes bibliographical references and index.
     Summary: A comprehensive reference work on the culture and history of Native Americans.
     ISBN 0-7614-0229-2 (vol. 2)   ISBN 0-7614-0227-6 (lib. bdg.: set)
     1. Indians of North America--Encyclopedias, Juvenile.
    [1. Indians of North America--Encyclopedias.]
    E76.2.E53   1997
    970.004'97'003--dc20

                                     96-7700
                                      CIP
                                      AC

Printed and bound in Italy

Title page illustration: A painting by Acee Blue Eagle, *Peace Pipe Dance*, depicts dancing and the smoking of a pipe in a Native American ceremony. For many tribes throughout the Americas, smoking tobacco in an ornamental pipe may be part of a celebratory ritual or a means of cleansing one's mind and body in preparation for an important meeting, conference, or conflict mediation.

Editor's note: Many systems of dating have been used by different cultures throughout history. *The Encyclopedia of North American Indians* uses B.C.E. (Before Common Era) and C.E. (Common Era) instead of B.C. (Before Christ) and A.D. (Anno Domini, "In the Year of Our Lord") out of respect for the diversity of the world's peoples.

Contents

BEADWORK AND BEADWORKERS

Native American glass beadwork is an original art form that combines materials of Native American and European cultures. These elements include such objects as Native wool cloth, tanned hide, and dyes and European beads, needles, and threads. Although Native peoples used shell beads prior to contact with Europeans, glass beads were first introduced to the Americas by Christopher Columbus (Cristóbal Colón) in the form of the larger necklace beads, which were popular trade items. Gradually, smaller beads were brought to the Americas, and beads became widely used for embroidered designs.

All glass beads came from Europe. Throughout the European colonizing of the Americas, beads were generally provided by the English, Dutch, and French, who obtained them from glassmakers in Venice, Italy. (The Spanish did not trade beads often, which explains why the people of the Southwest, who were influenced by Spaniards, did not develop beadwork as a popular artistic expression.) Glassmakers blew a bubble of molten glass on the end of a hollow tube. The hot bubble was then stretched into a long hollow rod of glass, which cooled. Next, the tubes were cut up into small sections, which were tumbled with sand to polish the newly created beads.

Prior to the development of glass beadwork, many Native peoples, such as the Lenapes, used wampum beads to decorate their clothing. In addition to embroidering wampum beads (also known as shell beads) onto their clothes, Native peoples used earth ochers as paint or dyed porcupine quills to decorate garments and objects made of hide— from moccasins to bags. The first glass beadwork imitated the older designs done in these dyes.

Beadwork by the peoples of the Northeast Woodlands and Great Lakes was done on Native-tanned leather in floral or lacy designs, often in imitation of European lace. Gradually, navy blue, scarlet, or black trade cloth made of fine wool was used as a common base for beadwork in the North-

Native American beadwork can be used for many purposes. Here, California Indians have decorated bottles and baskets with beads.

Today, Indian children are more likely to be encouraged to learn traditional art forms. In the past, schools discouraged such learning. The changes in education came about when Indian parents became involved in helping to plan culturally relevant programs for their children.

east. Originally, the beads were sewn to the hide (leather) using a fine piece of twisted sinew, which is a tendon from the spines of large animals, such as deer or moose. The holes in the hide were made with a finely sharpened awl made of bone. Later, Native beadworkers used steel or iron awls that they received in trade from the Europeans, followed by needles and linen or cotton thread.

Many different techniques evolved, producing various styles among different nations. Often, it is possible to tell which tribe created a certain piece of beadwork by either the techniques or the designs. It is also possible to know when certain beadwork was created because it changed with the times or because new colors of beads were introduced.

Beadwork is often thought of as a symbolic representation of things or beliefs, but this is not always the case. Often the designs were created just to be artistically or personally pleasing with little or no significance beyond their decorative importance. Traditional designs could be geometric, floral, or pictographic, meaning they depicted realistic scenes featuring animals or people. Beadwork that was symbolic usually had private significance, with the meanings known only to the owner or maker.

In the old days, almost all beadwork was done by women. If a man needed beaded items, such as a pipe bag, for instance, he would show the woman the designs he had perhaps dreamed. Thus, even the beadworker did not always know the full meaning of the designs she worked.

Today, many men are also fine beadworkers, and the range of designs varies from traditional to contemporary. Often, whimsical designs are used for children's items, such as a depiction of Mickey Mouse on a pair of moccasins. Other contemporary designs include such symbols as eagle feathers, buffalo skulls, or the four directions—all meaningful to Native Americans.

Some of the more popular techniques include lazy stitch, loom work, running back stitch, two-thread spot stitch, and peyote or gourd stitch. Lazy stitch is so called because the threads pass only through the top of the leather, not all the way through. Lazy stitch was used to cover broad areas with solid beadwork and no stitches showing on the inside that could wear out.

Loom work is a technique that weaves the beads between weft and warp threads. (The *warp* is the series of yarns or strings that extends lengthwise on the loom, crossed at right angles by the *weft*.) Loom work is often used by the Great Lakes nations to decorate strips or bags called bandoliers.

Running back stitch and two-thread spot stitch are used to create curved lines in floral designs. Running back stitch is a technique in which the beads are sewn down with the needle going back under the hide or fabric, then emerging in the middle of the beads to pass back through them, creating an unbroken line or direction of travel on a curved pattern. Two-thread spot stitch is similar, but the beads are gathered on a long thread and a second needle stitches them down to create a tight, curved line of beads.

Peyote or gourd stitch requires a lot of patience because only one bead is added at a time. This technique is named for its use in beading the handles of gourd rattles or other objects used in the peyote ceremony of the Native American Church. All of the above techniques are very time consuming, and beadwork is usually quite expensive. A fully beaded hide dress in 1995 would cost approximately five to ten thousand dollars.

Commonly beaded objects today include moccasins, cuffs, dresses, bags of all types, and regalia used for dance outfits at powwows. Beaded earrings, hair barrettes, belt buckles, caps, and even sneakers are popular modern examples of glass beadwork used in everyday life by Native people. Such forms of beadwork are also sold to support Native families.

Beadwork continues to grow in popularity as each generation of Native Americans continues to express traditional values in a modern world.

— J. Monture

SEE ALSO:
Jewelry, Native; Quillwork and Quillworkers; Wampum.

Beadwork designs are often created just to be artistically or personally pleasing, with little or no significance beyond their decorative importance. Symbolic beadwork usually has private significance, with the meanings known only to the owner or maker.

BEAR'S HEART, JAMES (1851–1882)

James Bear's Heart was also known as Nockkoist or Nacoista. He was a nineteenth-century Cheyenne warrior-artist who began creating drawings on ledger paper while imprisoned at Fort Marion in St. Augustine, Florida, following the Red River War on the Southern Plains. Born in 1851, Bear's Heart grew to adulthood pursuing the traditional ways of his people. As a warrior, he fought with tribal allies against Euro-American encroachments on Native lands.

Bear's Heart was arrested at Cheyenne Agency, in present-day Oklahoma, on April 3, 1875, and charged as an accomplice in the killing of a Euro-American family. Transported to Fort Marion for imprisonment, he and other prisoners of war were placed under the guard of military officer Captain Richard Henry Pratt. Pratt eventually released the hostages from their chains, trusted them to form their own guard, and began instructing them in Euro-American ways. Provided with ledger paper, Bear's Heart was among the prisoners who created drawings depicting scenes from tribal life.

After three years at Fort Marion, he and the other hostages were given a choice of returning home or staying in the East to continue their schooling in the "white man's road." Samuel Chapman Armstrong, the founder of Virginia's Hampton Normal and Agricultural Institute, had agreed to Pratt's proposal to enroll some of the former prisoners as students. Bear's Heart attended Hampton Institute from 1878 to 1881, the longest of any of the seventeen Fort Marion students who began at the school. During that period, he participated in study and work programs, assisted newly recruited Native students, served as an anniversary speaker, and continued to create artwork. Before returning home in 1881, Bear's Heart also served as color-bearer at the presidential inauguration of James A. Garfield. The warrior-artist died of scrofulous tuberculosis on January 25, 1882, at the Cheyenne-Arapaho Agency.

SEE ALSO:
Boarding Schools; Carlisle Indian School; Hampton Institute.

BEAVER WARS

The Beaver Wars were a series of wars conducted by the Iroquois on various fur-trading tribes of the Great Lakes region. The wars occurred from the 1630s through 1701 because of decreasing numbers of beaver in Iroquois territory and the subsequent Iroquois need for territory with plentiful beaver.

From the mid-sixteenth to the early seventeenth centuries, Algonquians and especially the Hurons were the main fur suppliers for the French fur trade. This particular movement of furs was disrupted by the Beaver Wars. The Iroquois, a confederacy established about 1560 and consisting of the Mohawks, Oneidas, Onondagas, Cayugas, and Senecas, were the main suppliers for the Dutch fur trade and were in competition with the French

and French-allied Indians throughout the seventeenth century.

The Beaver Wars began with Mohawk attacks on the Algonquians in the 1630s in their hopes of gaining French neutrality and unrestricted access to the areas north of the St. Lawrence valley. Beginning in the 1640s, the Mohawks also began attacking the Abenakis. By 1642, the Iroquois were beginning to raid Huron villages. They later attacked the Nipissings and Petuns, a tribe allied with the Hurons, in the winter of 1649–1650. In 1649, the Hurons were essentially defeated and dispersed, and by 1651, the Neutrals were defeated as well. Beginning in 1653 and lasting until 1657, the Iroquois attacked the Eries, who moved toward Chesapeake Bay and merged with the Iroquois by 1680. From 1659–1660, the Senecas, Cayugas, and Onondagas warred with the Susquehannocks despite their alliance with the Mohawks. Simultaneously, the Mohawks were warring with the Sokokis and Mahicans. These wars were interspersed with periods of negotiated peace with the French and the consequent establishment of French missions.

In 1680, the Senecas attacked the Illinois, which resulted in a series of French attacks on Iroquois villages. These French attacks included one on the Seneca in 1687, another against the Mohawks in 1693, and a final attack against the Onondagas and Oneidas in 1696. By 1701, the Iroquois were defeated by the French. In that year the Great Settlement was established, which provided Iroquois peace with Canada and Iroquois cession of hunting grounds west of Detroit.

Historians attribute the Beaver Wars to Iroquois economic dependence on Dutch goods, beginning in the 1630s and 1640s. When this dependence on European trade was combined with the decline in beavers in Iroquois territory, the Iroquois began desperately seeking other means of acquiring furs, such as territory with plentiful beaver populations. Indians were able to maintain control and power as long as there were several competing European powers. But when they became economically dependent on European goods and trade relationships, and when they lost the power to switch allies and traders to receive better goods, prices, and treatment, their ability to manipulate and control their futures was severely curtailed. The Beaver Wars, therefore, signify one of the early moments of a particular group of Indians struggling to retain autonomy and power.

SEE ALSO:
American Fur Company; Beavers; Hudson's Bay Company; North West Company.

BEAVERS

Beavers live in well-organized societies in and around lakes and streams in Canada and the United States. They build dams to form artificial ponds; they then build homes, called lodges, in the ponds. At the time of European contact with the Americas, beavers were plentiful. With the coming of European colonizers, beaver hats became fashionable in Europe. European traders hired trappers, including some Native Americans, who hunted beavers in such numbers that they nearly became extinct over large areas of North America.

Some authors argue that Native culture is no better than European culture at preserving the natural environment. They point to Native participation in the slaughter of the beaver and other fur-bearing animals for trade. In a controversial book, *Keepers of the Game,* Calvin Martin speculates that some Native peoples may have thought that beavers were carriers of European diseases and that the beaver was thus responsible for the incursions of Europeans.

Martin contends that the image of Native Americans as conservationists is just another stereotype. In his view, the fact of millions of dead beavers argues against the view that Native peoples generally held nature to be sacred and that most Natives took from nature only what they needed. As long as harvestable numbers of beavers remained, Native hunters worked with Europeans and Euro-Americans to kill as many

A Cree woman prepares a beaver for cooking. When properly prepared, beaver meat is delicious. Scent glands must be carefully removed.

animals as possible in the shortest time. But many Native people view Martin's book as part of a recent trend to discredit traditional Native culture. This trend has been growing since the beginnings of the modern antitreaty movement, which started after some tribes had their rights to practice traditional hunting and fishing methods upheld by the courts.

Native peoples did not begin the commercial fur trade on their own. They had lived in natural harmony with the beaver for thousands of years before Europe imposed mercantile capitalism on them. By the time of the fur trade, the Europeans' economy

A Cree man displays a catch of beaver pelts. Beavers are the most difficult fur-bearing animals in North America to skin. The pelt must be removed slowly and carefully, an inch at a time. The pelts are then stretched on rounded frames to dry.

was destroying more than the beaver population. Native societies themselves were being destroyed through the spread of trade goods, liquor, and disease, as well as the loss of hunting animals and land.

Native peoples during early contact with Europeans were trying to survive under rules imposed on them. Those who took part in the beaver trade often did so to acquire trade goods, which in turn created dependency and caused them to abandon traditional beliefs and methods of economy. Within their councils, beginning as early as 1700, Native peoples realized what was happening to them and debated whether European trade goods should be accepted at all. The fur trade was clearly a result of European intrusion in North America. If the European trading industry had not been introduced, the beaver would not have been hunted to near extinction.

Today, beavers have been reintroduced into many areas where their populations were once eliminated by trapping. Beaver restoration programs have been so successful that beavers are now considered a nuisance by some land users, who find that beaver dams flood roads, fields, and meadows. In many places, the beaver now has no natural enemies to keep its numbers in check. Thus, most states that have reintroduced the beaver into formerly depleted areas now allow trapping seasons for them each winter.

SEE ALSO:
American Fur Company; Beaver Wars; Hudson's Bay Company; North West Company.

BEDFORD, DENTON R. (1907–)

Denton R. Bedford is a contemporary American Indian novelist. He is mixed-blood Minsi (Munsee) and Anglo. Through his father, Sitamaganend, he is descended from Chief Wapalanewa, a famous pro-British ally during the American Revolution. Bedford, whose Minsi name is Wapalanewa, earned B.S. and M.S. degrees in history from Lafayette College in Pennsylvania and also did additional graduate work at Columbia University in New York City. Bedford taught both high school and college history and is the author of the novel *Tsali*, published in 1972. The novel takes place during the forced removal of the Cherokee people to Indian Territory (1830s) and is a fictionalized account of the authentic Cherokee hero, Tsali.

BELL, BETTY LOUISE (1949–)

Betty Louise Bell (Cherokee) is a novelist and scholar who was born near Davis, Oklahoma, and grew up in Oklahoma and California. She received a Ph.D. in English from Ohio State University and has taught at Ohio State University and the University of California at Berkeley.

In 1993, Bell taught the first course in Native American literature ever offered at Harvard. She is presently Assistant Professor of English, American Culture, and Women's Studies at the University of Michigan, where she is also director of the Native American Studies program.

Bell has been the recipient of an academic fellowship at the D'Arcy McNickle Center for the History of the American Indian at The Newberry Library in Chicago. She is a member of the Native Writers' Circle of the Americas and the Modern Language Association (MLA), and she serves as vice president of the Association for the Study of American Indian Literatures (ASAIL). ASAIL publishes the quarterly academic journal *Studies in American Indian Literatures* (*SAIL*) and *ASAIL NOTES*, a newsletter that reports on new publications in the field of Native American literature, as well as other related news.

In 1992, Bell participated in the historic gathering of nearly four hundred Native literary writers at the University of Oklahoma called Returning the Gift. At the 1993 convention of the Modern Language Association in Toronto, Bell organized a session that featured presentations on the poetry and fiction of Chickasaw novelist Linda Hogan.

Bell's work has been anthologized in *Aniyunwiya/Real Human Beings: An Anthology of Contemporary Cherokee Prose* (1995), edited by Joseph Bruchac. Bell's critically acclaimed first novel, *Faces in the Moon* (1994), tells the story

of three generations of contemporary Cherokee women—a woman caught between her mother and her grandmother, who each attach a different meaning to their Cherokee heritage. It is volume nine in the *American Indian Literature and Critical Studies* series of the University of Oklahoma Press.

SEE ALSO:
Returning the Gift.

BELLECOURT, CLYDE AND VERNON

The Bellecourt brothers, Clyde and Vernon, have long been active in the American Indian Movement (AIM). They continue to be leaders in the movement, especially in indigenous communities in the Minneapolis, Minnesota, area.

AIM leader Clyde Bellecourt is shown at a 1980 economic conference in Miami, Florida, where President Jimmy Carter announced a new youth job placement program.

AIM leader Vernon Bellecourt in 1973, addressing students at Kent State University at a memorial ceremony honoring four students who were killed on the campus on May 4, 1970.

1968. AIM was formed to fight for the rights of Indian people. As part of the movement, Clyde helped create the AIM Patrol, which followed the Minneapolis police and reduced arrests and harassment of Indians considerably. AIM also created programs in Minneapolis to help in the education, housing, and general welfare of the Indian population.

Clyde also founded the Legal Rights Center of Minneapolis and the South High Housing Project in Minneapolis (now known as Little Earth of United Tribes, Inc.). In 1972, he helped coordinate the Trail of Broken Treaties, which produced the Twenty Points position paper that was presented to the White House. In 1973, he became vice president of the National Alliance Party Against Racism and Political Repression. He took part in the occupation of Wounded Knee, South Dakota, that same year.

Clyde addressed the World Council of Churches in 1974 and was founder of an advocate agency for sixteen alternative schools for Indian children in 1975. He represented AIM in Geneva, Switzerland, during hearings on discrimination against indigenous peoples in 1977 and participated in the Longest Walk in 1978. He founded the American Indian Opportunities Industrialization Center (OIC) in Minneapolis in 1979 and became president of the OIC and cofounder of the Circle for Survival Consortium in 1980.

Vernon cofounded the Denver, Colorado, chapter of the American Indian Movement in 1970. In 1971, he faced indictments in Arizona for supporting indigenous groups in the Southwest that were trying to stop white community organizations

Clyde Bellecourt was born May 8, 1936, at White Earth Indian Hospital in Minnesota. Vernon Bellecourt was born at Menomeni, Minnesota. The brothers are members of the White Earth Chippewa, who are also known as Anishinabe or Ojibwe. The Bellecourts are of the Crane Clan and can trace their ancestry back to Chief White Crane.

Clyde was a founding member of the American Indian Movement, which began in Minneapolis in

from exploiting Native cultures, sacred songs, dances, and ceremonials in Flagstaff, Arizona. Vernon was appointed National Director of AIM by the movement's central council in 1972 and assisted in organizing and planning the Trail of Broken Treaties at a meeting in Denver that same year.

Vernon was indicted on conspiracy charges for the occupation of the Bureau of Indian Affairs building in Washington, D.C., which ended the Trail of Broken Treaties. He also participated in the demonstration held at Custer, South Dakota, which resulted in Indian people being assaulted by police.

Vernon was indicted by a federal grand jury on conspiracy charges involving the Wounded Knee occupation. The charges were dropped for lack of evidence. He was also arrested while supporting the Tuscarora-Lumbee Nation in the issue of Indian control of the nation's children.

Vernon organized and participated in the first International Indian Treaty Council conference in 1974. He helped draft the Declaration of Continuing Independence of the Sovereign Indian Nations. This helped set the course for Indian nations to take their cases of colonialism to the United Nations and other international forums.

Vernon represented AIM and the International Indian Treaty Council abroad on numerous occasions throughout the late 1970s and the 1980s. He also held the post of secretary-treasurer of the White Earth Anishinabe Governing Council. In the 1990s, Vernon founded the National Coalition on Racism in Sports and Media and has fought to eliminate stereotypes and negative caricatures of Indians in mainstream society.

Internal divisiveness within AIM, which began as early as 1988, came to a head in 1994 when a group of long-time activists, including Russell Means and Robert Robideau, assembled in New Mexico and agreed to the Edgewood Declaration of the International Confederation of the Autonomous Chapters of the American Indian Movement. The confederation leveled several charges against the Bellecourt brothers, including charges of undermining or corrupting the leadership of AIM. A tribunal was conducted, and Clyde and Vernon were found guilty of several charges. The Bellecourts, however, dispute the proceedings.

The split within AIM widened, and it seemed doubtful that the two sides could ever reconcile their differences. However, Joe Locust, who cofounded Denver AIM with Vernon, was a panelist during the confederation tribunal. Locust has predicted that when a major crisis happens, the two sides within AIM will join forces again, and the infighting of the late 1980s and early 1990s will be forgotten. And despite the charges against the Bellecourts, the confederation has stated that the work Clyde and Vernon have done for Indian people cannot be forgotten.

"I do not have one ounce of patriotism for the U.S. government," Vernon Bellecourt has said. "I am a patriot for the cause of oppressed people. And I am a citizen of the sovereign White Earth Indigenous Nation."

— S. S. Davis

SEE ALSO:
American Indian Movement; Longest Walk; Trail of Broken Treaties; Wounded Knee, Confrontation at (1973).

BENDER, CHARLES ALBERT
(1883–1954)

A pitcher with a fastball that was said to rival that of the renowned Walter Johnson, Charles Albert Bender was elected to the Baseball Hall of Fame at Cooperstown, New York, in 1953.

Born of mixed parentage near Brainerd, Minnesota, in the Bad River Band of the Ojibwe (also known as Chippewa and Anishinabe), Bender attended Carlisle Indian School and earned a degree at Dickinson College. He began his major-league baseball career in 1903 with the Philadelphia Athletics. During a dozen years under manager Connie Mack, Athletics teams won the American League pennant five times and the World Series three times. Bender was recognized as the best pitcher on the team, and he led the league in strikeouts in 1910, 1911, and 1914. Some Philadelphia sportswriters called Bender "Connie Mack's meal ticket."

After 1914, Bender played a year for Baltimore in the short-lived Federal League and then two more years for the Philadelphia Nationals. During his major-league career, Bender won 200 games and lost 111. Occasionally, fans of other teams would

Charles Bender as a member of the Philadelphia Athletics at the Polo Grounds, New York, September 13, 1914. A member of the Bad River Band of the Ojibwe, Bender was elected to the Baseball Hall of Fame in 1953.

deride his ancestry. Bender's response was to call them "foreigners." When one fan remarked that she thought all Indians wore feathers, Bender quipped, "We do, madam, but this happens to be molting season."

Later in life, Bender worked as a baseball coach at the U.S. Naval Academy as well as for the Chicago White Sox and his old team, the Philadelphia Athletics. A year after he was elected to the Baseball Hall of Fame, Bender died of cancer.

SEE ALSO:
Baseball; Carlisle Indian School.

BENSON, DIANE

Diane Benson (Tlingit) is a playwright, poet, lecturer, actress, and director whose 'Tak'deintaan (Tlingit) name is Lxeis. She is of the Sea Tern Clan and grew up in southeast Alaska near Sitka. She has operated a talent agency, Northern Stars, which primarily represents people of color, most of whom are Native Alaskans. She has also lived in Chugiak, where she ran dog teams for fun and handled them for her son, who runs them competitively. Recently she directed a play, *Ecstasy of Rita Joe,* for the University of Alaska Mainstage. As an Artist in the School under the Alaska State Arts Council, she teaches theater workshops for children.

She has said of her childhood that she grew up "amid the struggle of Indian survival" and that this forms the core of her work. As an actress, she possesses a dynamic and captivating stage presence. She performed scenes from her play "Sister Warrior" at the Returning the Gift conference at the University of Oklahoma in 1992. In 1994, at the Pacific Northwest regional Returning the Gift conference at Cape Flattery Resort on the Makah Reservation in Washington state, she teamed with noted Native theater promoter Ken Jackson (Gray Eagle) and others in presenting a workshop on Native American theater, and she shared the story of her life and how it relates to her professional work on a panel discussing issues relating to Native identity.

Her poetry has appeared in such publications and anthologies as *AL-ESK-IND, Sovereign Indigenous Women of the Arctic Newsletter,* and *Raven Tells Stories* (1991); the "Native American Literatures" special issue of *Callaloo* (1994); and *Returning the Gift: Poetry and Prose from the First North American Native Writers' Festival* (1994).

SEE ALSO:
Returning the Gift.

BENTON-BANAI, EDWARD J.
(1934–)

Native educator Edward J. Benton-Banai was born March 4, 1934, at Stone Lake on the Lac Courte Oreilles Ojibwe Reservation in Wisconsin. He is a full-blooded Lac Courte Oreilles (LCO) Band member of the Lake Superior Ojibwe (also spelled *Ojibwa*), who are also known as Anishinabe or Chippewa.

Benton-Banai's Anishinabe name is Baw Dway Wi Dun, meaning "the Messenger." Benton-Banai grew up in a village where people had withdrawn specifically to keep to traditional cultural lifeways and the Anishinabe language. His mother allowed no English spoken in the home, and so he learned English in school. After a Korean War stint as an army paratrooper, he worked as a high-bridge steelworker.

In 1968, Benton-Banai became involved with Indian education at the first Native Survival School, which was formed by Indian parents in Minneapolis, Minnesota. Education has been his life's mission ever since, including (when necessary) participation in occupations or takeovers of vacant premises to demonstrate the need for school funds and facilities.

In 1972, Benton-Banai founded Red School House in the shabby quarters of an abandoned parochial school in St. Paul, Minnesota. Red School House is controlled entirely by Indian parents and community representatives. Benton-Banai took the lead in encouraging the Native teaching staff to obtain degrees required for school certification. In 1978, he received a bachelor of science degree in education from the University of Minnesota—a degree he obtained through after-hours study.

Benton-Banai used his example to demonstrate to Native teaching staff that degrees could be earned

Edward J. Benton-Banai at a 1993 powwow in Wisconsin. Benton-Banai is a leader in the field of American Indian education.

in this way. He then organized through local colleges the Native American Educational Leadership Program, which offered degrees to Native educators with daytime jobs.

Red School House is an American Indian Movement (AIM) Survival School. Its students were punished by an abrupt cutoff in the school's modest federal funding in 1973. This cutoff was the government's retaliation for the AIM protest and occupation of Wounded Knee, South Dakota. The U.S. Supreme Court decision that eventually restored funding called the cutoff "making war on Indian children."

Red School House has been a model for Native educators for its unique ways of combining the traditional with the best of the new. Although there was never much funding, Red School House began computer education for its students in 1980. An Ojibwe vocabulary-teaching program was prepared using the Apple II computer in 1983. Pipe ceremonies, cedar and sage smudging, sweat lodges, drum and dance, student and parent preparation of crafts and regalia, and understanding of the historical and cultural background of Native people—all these have been central to Benton-Banai's educational efforts. However, he also has been a leader in envisioning how to include the best aspects of technology in culturally relevant Native education.

Benton-Banai has held educational leadership positions for the Saginaw Tribe, the Menominee Tribe of Wisconsin, and the Lac Courte Oreilles Ojibwe School. In the early 1990s, he created a visionary program integrating culturally based education in all subjects at Heart of the Earth Survival School in Minneapolis, Minnesota. He also revitalized Red School House, whose program had fallen into difficulties after he left it in the mid-1980s.

Benton-Banai is a fourth-degree Midewiwin Initiate, Water Drum-Keeper, and Pipe Carrier. He serves as Officer and Grand Chief of the Three Fires Society, which sponsors traditional Mide spiritual ceremonies among tribespeople of the Great Lakes region.

Benton-Banai travels to conduct Midewiwin ceremonies, and he provides spiritual guidance to young people through his life example and school practices, as well as his through the strength of his personality. Benton-Banai has written books for young children and teenagers that tell traditional, sacred, and historic stories. He has received many awards and is in demand as a consultant on Native education.

SEE ALSO:

American Indian Movement; Wounded Knee, Confrontation at (1973).

"Dance to the Berdache," George Catlin's depiction of a Sac and Fox ceremony. Many traditional Native American cultures accept sexual divergence as an indication that a person can be two-spirited. Europeans were not tolerant of these views and sought to suppress them.

BERDACHE

Walter William's book *The Spirit and the Flesh* and Will Roscoe's book *Living the Spirit* both document historical evidence for the existence of specific social and ceremonial roles that respect gays in some traditional Native American cultures. *Berdache* (a word that was first applied to American Indian homosexuals by French travelers and explorers in the eighteenth century) is a term in contemporary literature that has come to be associated with these roles.

In some traditional cultures, gay people are believed to be two-spirited, that is, that they are between genders and are therefore capable of seeing from both the male world and the female world and thus blessed with a double portion of power. In these tribes—because of their in-between status in terms of gender—gays are believed to be especially powerful in positions of mediation, including spiritual roles that require judgment in both the natural and supernatural worlds.

Traditionally, not every Native American tribe accepted homosexuality, yet there is a substantial body of cross-tribal evidence that shows that many did. Contemporary Indian communities are often as homophobic (fearful of homosexuality) as their non-Indian counterparts, yet among some traditional Native people the respected tribal roles are remembered. Contemporary Native gays and lesbians have begun to reexamine their traditions and to imagine themselves as two spirits, rather than accept the way dominant culture often shames gays and lesbians and fragments their lives.

This reexamination has led to the formation of such groups as Gay American Indians (GAI), founded in San Francisco in 1975 by Randy Burns (Northern Paiute) and Barbara Cameron (Lakota), as well as groups in Minneapolis and New York City and other cities with large gay communities and urban Indian populations.

SEE ALSO:
Homosexuality.

BERINGIA

The Bering Strait is a narrow stretch of water separating North America from Asia. It is believed that thousands of years ago, the Bering Strait was dry and that instead of a stretch of water between Alaska and Siberia were grasslands with scattered shrubs, and possibly small trees, covering gently rolling hills, with small ponds and lakes. Herds of caribou, mammoths, mastodons, and other animals roamed freely. This dry land between Asia and North America is called Beringia, or the Bering Land Bridge.

Although there is some dispute within many Native cultures about whether Beringia actually existed, scientists say that it would have existed during the last ice age, a period that stretched over thousands of years and ended about ten thousand years ago. In an ice age, low global temperatures cause waters that normally would flow into oceans to freeze into huge sheets of ice, called glaciers. During the last ice age, much of North America was buried under glaciers. With so much water frozen in the glaciers, the oceans became smaller. In fact, ocean levels may have been as much as 350 feet (106 meters) lower than they are today. Areas that had once been covered by shallow seas dried up. This is how Beringia would have been formed.

Although it is called a land bridge, the exposed land was hardly what we think of as a bridge. At its largest, Beringia was probably 800 to 1,000 miles (1,300 to 1,600 kilometers) wide and nearly 250,000 square miles (650,000 square kilometers) in area—a mass larger than many states combined.

Archaeological evidence suggests that people may have crossed the land bridge at many different times, some very early, some quite late. Scientists are not certain when the earliest migration might have occurred or how many migrations there might have been. Some artifacts hint that people may have crossed the land bridge as much as thirty thousand years ago. It is likely that by twenty thousand years ago, both people and animals were able to pass back and forth between North America and Asia.

Some archaeologists believe that the first people to live in the Americas arrived during that time. Many traditional Native cultures believe that people have lived in the Americas for at least two hundred thousand years. Many Native cultures have creation stories that tell of their people being created in their homelands. They say that they have always been here, and that the existence of Beringia is irrelevant to their presence in the Americas.

If Beringia ever existed, it disappeared beneath the Bering Strait ten thousand years ago, when the earth began to warm and the glaciers melted.

SEE ALSO:
Archaic Period.

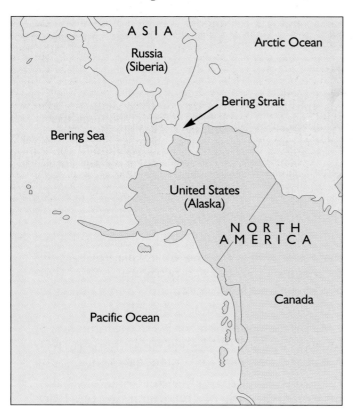

It is widely believed that a land "bridge" between Asia and North America existed in the distant past, during an interglacial epoch, when ocean levels were lower. Some Native cultures disagree with scientists about when—and whether—this occurred.

BIGEAGLE, DUANE (1946–)

Duane BigEagle (Osage) is a widely published poet and educator who is also a painter, community organizer, and cultural activist. Currently living in Petaluma, California, he was born at the Indian Hospital in Claremore, Oklahoma, in May 1946, the grandson of a full-blood Osage grandfather. He received a B.A. degree from the University of California at Berkeley, having been the recipient of a Santa Fe Foundation scholarship. He has taught creative writing for nearly twenty years through the California Poets in the Schools program, for which he has also served as statewide Affirmative Action Coordinator and president of the board of directors. He has also been a lecturer in American Indian Studies at San Francisco State University.

His books of poetry include *Bidato* (1975) and *Birthplace: Poems and Paintings* (1983). His work has appeared in many publications, including *The Chicago Review*, *The Nation*, *Sun Tracks*, and *Florida Quarterly*. His work has been anthologized in many collections, including *The Remembered Earth: An Anthology of Contemporary Native American Literature*, edited by Geary Hobson (1979 and 1980), *Songs from this Earth on Turtle's Back*, edited by Joseph Bruchac (1983), *Durable Breath: Contemporary Native American Poetry*, edited by John E. Smelcer and D. L. Birchfield (1994), and *Returning the Gift: Poetry and Prose from the First North American Native Writers' Festival*, also edited by Joseph Bruchac (1994).

At Returning the Gift, a conference of nearly four hundred Native literary writers at the University of Oklahoma in 1992, BigEagle participated on a panel discussion titled "Writing for Our Children," and he helped conduct a workshop on the topic of "Bringing Native Writing to Our Schools." He is a member of the Native Writers' Circle of the Americas, a professional association of Native literary writers, which was formed at the Returning the Gift conference. He also serves as a

Osage poet Duane BigEagle has worked for more than twenty years in the California Poets in the Schools program. His poetry has appeared in many publications and anthologies.

mentor in Wordcraft Circle of Native American Mentor and Apprentice Writers, also formed at the Returning the Gift conference, which helps beginning and emerging Native literary writers learn their craft and find publication outlets for their work.

SEE ALSO:
Returning the Gift.

BIG ELK (c. 1765–1853)

Big Elk (Ongpatonga) became principal chief of the Omaha on the death of Black Bird (Washing-gusaba) in 1800. In 1821 and 1837, Big Elk traveled to Washington, D.C., to negotiate treaties, and he became known among whites as a spellbinding orator. He was the principal Omaha chief at the time of the first sizable European-American migration through Omaha territory; the newcomers were Mormons traveling from Illinois to their eventual destination on the shores of the Great Salt Lake.

Big Elk, here depicted in an engraving by Hugh Bridport based on a painting by J. Neagle, was principal chief of the Omahas from 1800 to 1843.

Big Elk was probably born in the main village of the U'maha (which has been anglicized as *Omaha*) midway between the present cities of Omaha, Nebraska, and Sioux City, Iowa. He earned a reputation for courage in war, primarily against the Pawnee, as a young man. He became very popular and was known for his fairness in making decisions, unlike Black Bird, a tyrant who was said to have poisoned some warriors who disagreed with him.

Charles Bird King painted Big Elk's portrait in Washington, D.C., during his first visit in 1821. George Catlin painted another portrait of Big Elk in 1833.

Big Elk was principal chief of the Omaha until 1843, when he was succeeded by Big Elk, the younger. Joseph LaFlesche followed Big Elk, the younger, as principal chief.

SEE ALSO:
Omaha.

BIG FOOT (1825–1890)

Big Foot, or *Siha-Tanka*, was chief of the Minniconjou Lakotas, of the Sioux nation, on the Cheyenne River Reservation in the late nineteenth century. Among his people he was known as a peaceful diplomat who often said, "I will stand in peace till my last day comes." But to the U.S. Army he was considered the last remaining "troublemaker" after the deaths of Sitting Bull and Crazy Horse.

In 1890, Big Foot left the Cheyenne River Reservation with three hundred of his Minniconjou people, and the army sent a detachment of the Eighth Cavalry, led by Lieutenant Col. Edwin Sumner, to track his movements and arrest him if he did not return to the agency.

The frozen body of Big Foot lies in a field at Wounded Knee, South Dakota. Big Foot was chief of the Minniconjou Lakotas of the Sioux nation when he and 143 of his people were massacred by the army on December 29, 1890.

During this time, Big Foot's band had been joined by more than three dozen of Sitting Bull's followers, who had fled the Standing Rock agency after the death of their great chief in mid-December 1890. Big Foot, fearing that he and his people might meet a similar fate, decided to journey to Pine Ridge, where Red Cloud, the Oglala chief, was on good terms with the U.S. government.

During the journey to Pine Ridge, Big Foot, who was traveling in a wagon, was suffering from pneumonia. Matters turned worse when they ran out of food. Big Foot knew that they could not continue to travel very much farther. The group was intercepted by soldiers of the Seventh Cavalry, Custer's old outfit, some of them veterans of the recent campaigns against the Sioux.

This was an unfortunate meeting, as many soldiers saw this as a chance to settle an old score, the death of Custer and his men at the Battle of the Little Bighorn. The Big Foot band was without arms except for a few outmoded guns, and the band consisted for the most part of old people, women, and children.

Through an interpreter, Big Foot explained to Major Samuel Whitside that he and his band were traveling to the Pine Ridge Agency to give themselves up. He also explained that they did not plan to cause any trouble. Whitside told Big Foot that he and his band would be allowed to continue their journey to Pine Ridge the next day, but for the evening, they must camp at Wounded Knee, which the Sioux called *Chankpe Opi Wakpala*. Wounded Knee is about twenty miles (thirty-two kilometers) from the Pine Ridge Agency, but the cavalry had no intention of sending Big Foot's band to Pine Ridge. Major Whitside had received an order that the Minniconjous were to be marched to Nebraska and loaded onto a train bound for Omaha—and prison.

During the night, the Minniconjous held a Ghost Dance, as more of the Seventh Cavalry arrived from Pine Ridge and Col. James Forsyth took over command. The practice of Indian religions, such as the Ghost Dance, had been made a crime by the government of the United States. The practice of Indian religions would remain a crime in the United States for nearly one hundred years, and the terror of what was about to happen to Big Foot's band, as news of the event spread throughout the continent, would play an important role in stopping the open practice of many Indian religions for many years.

Col. Forsyth did not have any prior experience engaging with Indians, and many of his enlisted men were new recruits. This fact may have accounted for the disaster that occurred the following morning, which U.S. historians referred to for many decades as the "Battle" of Wounded Knee. It was there that Chief Big Foot met his tragic fate. He died along with 153 Sioux men, women, and children, on December 29, 1890, when the army shot them down. The Minniconjous were buried in a mass grave at Wounded Knee, which is now a memorial on the Pine Ridge Reservation.

Recently, many Lakotas have conducted a ceremonial ride in mid-winter to commemorate the Wounded Knee massacre and to complete the rituals they were not allowed to carry out in 1890.

SEE ALSO:
Crazy Horse; Little Bighorn, Battle of the; Custer, George Armstrong; Ghost Dance Religion; Siouan Nations; Sitting Bull; Wounded Knee (1890).

BIG HOUSE CHURCH

The term *Big House Church* refers to the building where the Lenape, also known as the Delaware, held their most sacred religious ceremony every autumn. *Big House* is a literal translation of *Xingwikaon*, the Lenape name for the building. The Lenape believe their religion was given to them when God gave churches to all nations so they could live good lives and be with God.

The ceremony at the Big House Church was held for twelve nights. It was said that the reason they had twelve nights is that they believed the sky is divided into twelve tiers and the Supreme Being is in the twelfth tier. In the ceremony, prayers were offered to God in thanks for the harvest and to ask for his blessings to be on all people for the forthcoming year. Many of the Lenapes who participated in the ceremony at the Big House Church lived a great distance away, and so they camped near the church throughout the time of the meeting.

The Big House Church was made of logs and was about 25 feet (7.5 meters) wide north to south and 40 feet (12 meters) long east to west. The roof had two large openings to allow the smoke to go out, and it was supported in the center of the building by a center post. On the center post, two large faces were carved, one that faced the east and one that faced the west. There were also three smaller faces on the north wall and three on the south wall. Two more faces were on the doorposts of the east door and two on the west doorposts. These were said to be the face of Mësingw, who was the guardian spirit of the game animals. There was also a man who was picked to impersonate the Mësingw. He wore a carved, wooden mask and a suit of bearskin and had an integral part in the ceremony.

The people attending the meeting used only the east door. The west door was opened only for the ceremonial attendants to take out the ashes from the old fire on the nights when a new fire was built. Within the church were specific places to sit for the members of the three Lenape clans—Wolf, Turtle, and Turkey. Not only were the clans seated separately, but the men and women also sat separately within special clan-designated areas.

In addition to the prayers to God, the ceremony also gave Lenapes a chance to tell of the visions they had in their younger days. These visions were said to have come to the young people during vision quests for the boys or a time of great anguish for the girls, and the visions came from a guardian spirit who took pity on the young person and came to be of help.

The last full Big House meeting was held west of Copan, Oklahoma, in 1924. It was discontinued because the visionaries were growing older and many had died; the younger people could not be sent on vision quests; the deer that were hunted to feed the participants had all been killed out; and the schools would not permit Indian children to miss school for twelve days to attend what the teachers considered a pagan ceremony. There was an attempt to revive the ceremony during World War II to pray for the safe return of the Lenape soldiers and for peace in the world, and an abbreviated ceremony was held three times at a Lenape home north of Dewey, Oklahoma.

No trace of the Big House remains, and the Lenape elders have said that now it must never be rebuilt. There is to be no revival of the songs, they say, for these songs belonged to the individuals who are now gone. They say this is the way it must be.

SEE ALSO:
Creation Stories.

SUGGESTED READINGS:
Elkhair, Charles. "Account of the Delaware Meeting House." Recorded by Truman Michelson (1912). Unpublished manuscript (NAA 2776) in the Smithsonian Institution.
Speck, Frank G. A Study of the Delaware Indian Big House Ceremony. Harrisburg: Pennsylvania Historical Commission, 1931.
Sumpter, Nancy Falleaf. "A Visit to the Meeting House." Bulletin of the Archaeological Society of New Jersey, No. 49 (1994), p. 60.

BIG SNAKE (d. 1879)

In 1877, in Omaha, Nebraska, the U.S. Army began forcing the Poncas, one of whose leaders was Standing Bear, to move southward. The Poncas had arrived in the Omaha area after marching on foot from Oklahoma in the winter. In order to survive the march, they were forced to eat first their horses and then their moccasins. They arrived in Omaha with their feet bleeding in the snow.

When non-Indian residents of Omaha learned of the army's order that the Poncas make yet another trek, many local citizens took an interest in the situation for humanitarian reasons and objected to the forced relocation. These citizens conducted a newspaper campaign in support of Standing Bear and sought a ruling on the order from Federal Judge Elmer Dundy. Dundy ruled that the army had acted inappropriately in Standing Bear's case, and he denied the army the power to forcibly relocate the Indians. The year of his ruling was 1879, however, and the U.S. government was at that time conducting many "Indian wars" against Native people. Dundy was concerned that his decision would cast doubt on the legality of *all* actions taken by the government against Native people, and so he was careful to word his ruling so that it applied only to Standing Bear and his party, and not to all Indians.

Big Snake, the brother of Standing Bear, was unaware of how strictly Dundy had worded his decision and decided to test the ruling by moving roughly 100 miles (160 kilometers) within Indian Territory (later Oklahoma), from the Poncas' assigned reservation to one occupied by Cheyennes. Because he was not a member of Standing Bear's party and was thus in violation of the judge's ruling, Big Snake was arrested by troops and returned to the Ponca reservation.

On October 31, 1879, Ponca Indian Agent William H. Whiteman called Big Snake a troublemaker and ordered a detail to imprison him. When Big Snake refused to surrender, insisting that he had committed no crime, he was shot to death.

In a statement to Congress, the Ponca Hairy Bear said that Big Snake asked the agents who came to arrest him what he had done wrong. "He said he had killed no one, stolen no horses, and that he had done no wrong," Hairy Bear testified. Big Snake told the agents that he carried no knife, "and he threw off his blanket and turned around to show that he had no weapon."

Big Snake refused to go, and an officer tried to arrest him forcibly. Big Snake fought off several such attempts from a sitting position. After that, six soldiers came at Big Snake and beat him with their rifle butts. Hairy Bear recalled, "It knocked him back to the wall. He straightened up again. The blood was running down his face. I saw the gun pointed at him, and was scared, and did not want to see him killed. So I turned away. Then the gun was fired and Big Snake fell down dead on the floor."

SEE ALSO:
Ponca; Standing Bear, Luther.

BILL C-31

In 1985, the federal government of Canada amended the Indian Act of 1876 to rectify certain forms of discrimination against Indian people in terms of their Indian status or registration. Initially, this act discriminated against Indian women who married non-Indians, as well as their descendants, by removing them from their band list and deleting them from the Indian list of Indian Affairs. Bill C-31 returned status to those who were denied or lost their status under provisions of the first Indian Act.

Bill C-31 also reenfranchised, or returned Indian status to, those who had lost their Indian status by voluntary surrender, leaving the reserve for more than five years, or completing a university degree or professional training. The bill permitted those who had lost their status through sexual discrimination or marriage to a non-Native person to apply for reenfranchisement.

Bill C-31 also provided for local control of alcoholic intoxicants. Prior to Bill C-31, intoxicants were forbidden by law unless they were bought under provincial laws. The bill allowed these substances to be controlled by local bylaws and gave the reserves the right to vote on the control and use of alcohol.

Finally, Bill C-31 increased the power of Native bands to resolve issues concerning their membership. The bill gave band councils the right to make laws regarding the residence of band members, regulation of rights of nonband members living or working on reserves, and the power to review decisions on band membership. In summary, the bill gave opportunities to strengthen Indian self-government in Canada.

SEE ALSO:
Canada, Native–Non-Native Relations in.

BINGO

SEE Gaming.

BIRD, GLORIA (1951–)

Gloria Bird (Spokane) was born in Sunnyside, Washington, in the Yakima Valley. She grew up on the Spokane Reservation and on the adjoining Colville Reservation. She is an accomplished poet, essayist, and teacher of creative writing. She attended reservation mission schools, as well as boarding schools operated by the Bureau of Indian Affairs, before studying at the Institute of American Indian Arts in Santa Fe, New Mexico, where she majored in creative writing. She received a B.A. in English from Lewis and Clark College in Portland, Oregon, and an M.A. in literature from the University of Arizona. She has now returned to New Mexico, where she teaches creative writing and literature at the Institute of American Indian Arts. Her mother lives at Nespelem, on the Colville Reservation in Washington, which Bird returns to frequently and considers her second home.

In the mid-1980s, she was one of the founding members of the Northwest Native American Writers Association (along with Elizabeth Woody, Ed Edmo, Vincent Wannassy, Philip Minthorn, and others). In 1988, she received a writer's grant from the Oregon Institute of Literary Arts.

In 1992, Bird shared the inaugural Diane Decorah Memorial Poetry Award as co-winner of the First Book Awards competition in poetry. This award was sponsored by Returning the Gift, a historic conference of nearly four hundred Native literary writers from throughout the upper Western Hemisphere that met at the University of Oklahoma in 1992. Bird's winning poetry manuscript, entitled *Full Moon Over the Reservation*, was published in 1993 by Greenfield Review Press.

As an essayist, Bird has made insightful observations about the colonization of Indians as an ongoing process, as much alive today as at any time in the past (in *Pacific Northwest Writer's Guide*, 1992). Since the early 1970s, her work has appeared in a number of publications, such as *High Plains Literary Review*, and in Native American special issues of *Fireweed*, *Mr. Cogito*, and others.

She is anthologized in such collections as *The American Indian Reader* (1973); *Dancing on the Rim of the World: An Anthology of Contemporary Northwest Native American Writing* (1990); *Talking Leaves: Contemporary Native American Short Stories* (1990); *Returning the Gift: Poetry and Prose from the First North American Native Writers' Festival* (1994), and others.

SEE ALSO:
Returning the Gift.

BLACK ELK (1863–1950)

Black Elk (Oglala Sioux), also known as Hehaka Sapa, is recognized for many things. He was a visionary, a prophet, and a holy man. He also witnessed some of the most horrific battles that occurred in the last part of the nineteenth century. Black Elk survived to tell about them in an autobiography titled *Black Elk Speaks, Being the Life Story of a Holy Man of the Oglala Sioux*. This important book was first published in 1932 through a collaborative effort with the poet John G. Neihardt. Black Elk's testimony became one of the most widely read literary classics of the twentieth century and is one of the most notable autobiographical accounts of American Indian life.

Black Elk was a member of the Oglala band of the Lakota nation. His father was a medicine man, and Black Elk was also a cousin of the famous Lakota warrior Crazy Horse. Black Elk was born near the eastern end of the border between Wyoming and Montana in a place the Lakota called the Little Powder River, during the winter of 1863, or in the Moon of the Popping Trees (December). At that time, there was much unrest for the Sioux people because settlers, soldiers, and gold seekers were invading the Indian lands, disturbing forever the Plains Indians' traditional ways of life.

At the age of nine, Black Elk fell unconscious for twelve days. Upon awakening, he recalled experiencing a great vision. This vision was one of many that had begun early in Black Elk's life. These visions indicated that Black Elk had been granted special powers by the Six Grandfathers, who were the spirits of the sky, earth, and the four directions. His vision offered him a painful glance into the future and what lay in store for his people. Black Elk did not tell of his vision for several years, for its meaning had disturbed and troubled him to such a degree. And still being a young boy, he could not fully comprehend the frightening vision nor understand what the Grandfather Spirits had given him.

Black Elk, a spiritual leader of the Oglala Sioux, witnessed many of the battles on the Northern Plains in the late nineteenth century. His autobiography, *Black Elk Speaks*, first published in 1932, is a literary classic.

Black Elk was thirteen years old during the time of the famous Battle of the Little Bighorn in southern Montana. This battle was a proud triumph for the Lakota, Arapaho, Blackfeet, and Cheyenne people, a day of victory in the Plains people's long struggle to defend their ancestral lands. It was also the site of the death of Lt. Colonel George Armstrong Custer, a much-celebrated Indian fighter and the leader of the U.S. Seventh Cavalry.

In his autobiography, Black Elk recounts the Battle of the Little Bighorn in the chapter titled "The Rubbing Out of Long Hair." In this chapter, he tells of collecting his first scalp from a dying soldier. He relates in vivid detail the many events that led up to the victory for the Indian people that day on the battlefield in the region they called Greasy Grass. Black Elk's account also tells of his cousin Crazy Horse's heroic acts, leadership, and bravery and of Crazy Horse's tragic death at the hand of the military soldiers.

When Black Elk was fifteen, he and many other Lakotas were forced to flee to Canada. They left their homelands in order to save their lives because U.S. Army troops, out for revenge, were pouring into their region. In Canadian country, the Lakotas knew they would find safety under the guidance of the Hunkpapa leaders Sitting Bull and Gall.

As he grew to adulthood, Black Elk's powers continued to increase. He became more aware that he should begin fulfilling the duties that the Grandfather Spirits had instructed him to perform. Black Elk carried an enormous responsibility, that of "bringing to life the flowering tree of his people," as he writes in his autobiography. This mission brought him much suffering and personal sacrifice, but he knew it must be carried out so that the the spiritual ways of the Lakota people could be restored and preserved.

Among his gifts were healing the sick and offering spiritual advice. He underwent many different ceremonies, including the Heyoka and the Elk Ceremony. It was those rites, and others, that gave Black Elk his knowledge about curing those who were ill.

Eventually, Black Elk and the other Lakotas who had fled to Canada returned to reservations in the United States. In 1886, when Black Elk was twenty-three, he journeyed to Europe, where he spent three years touring with Buffalo Bill's Wild West Show. This spectacular show traveled throughout Italy, Germany, France, and England, where Black Elk received the honor of meeting Queen Victoria.

While he was in France, however, Black Elk became seriously ill and experienced another vision that caused him to return to the United States and to his people. Back at the Pine Ridge Reservation in South Dakota, he discovered that his people were starving. He also learned that a Paiute prophet named Wovoka was spreading the Ghost Dance Religion. This new religion promised the return of the buffalo and a recovery of the traditional Indian way of life. It came to a devastating end, however, in the winter of 1890 with the massacre at Wounded Knee.

Many years later, in 1932, the poet John G. Neihardt recorded Black Elk's life story in the book *Black Elk Speaks*. In the dedication to this book, Black Elk writes, "What is good in this book is given back to the Six Grandfathers and to the great men of my people." Black Elk lived to be eighty-seven years old, but his words will live on forever.

— T. Midge

SEE ALSO:

Buffalo Bill's Wild West Show; Crazy Horse; Custer, George Armstrong; Gall; Ghost Dance Religion; Little Bighorn, Battle of the; Sitting Bull; Wounded Knee (1890).

SUGGESTED READINGS:

Avery, Susan, and Linda Skinner. *Extraordinary American Indians*. Chicago: Childrens Press, 1992.

Black Elk, Wallace, and William S. Lyon. *Black Elk: The Sacred Ways of the Lakota*. New York: HarperCollins Publishers, Inc., 1990.

Brown, Dee. *Bury My Heart at Wounded Knee*. New York: Henry Holt and Company, 1970.

DeMallie, Raymond J., ed. *The Sixth Grandfather: Black Elk's Teachings Given to John G. Neihardt*. Lincoln: University of Nebraska Press, 1984.

Erdoes, Richard. *Crying for a Dream: The World Through Native American Eyes*. Santa Fe: Bear and Company Publishing, 1989.

Neihardt, John G. *Black Elk Speaks*. Lincoln: University of Nebraska Press, 1932.

BLACK HAWK
(1767–1838)

Black Hawk, also known as Makataimeshekiakiak, was a member of the Thunder Clan of the Sauk Nation. He won renown as a warrior from the time he first participated in warfare at the age of fifteen to the time of his leadership of the Native rebellion of 1832, known as the Black Hawk War.

About 1820, the Fox and Sauk were divided over whether to resist Euro-American expansion into their country, in what is now southern Illinois. Keokuk and a number of his supporters decided to accommodate the expansion, and they moved into what is now Iowa. Black Hawk and his supporters remained at their principal village, Saukenuk, at the confluence of the Rock and Mississippi Rivers. This was the site of present-day Rock Island, Illinois. The land provided abundant crops, and the river was a rich source of fish. Black Hawk consulted with the spiritual leaders White Cloud and Neapope, who advised him to seek allies in defense of their land.

In the meantime, George Davenport, Indian agent in the area, had purchased the site on which Saukenuk was built. His purchase included Black Hawk's own lodge and his people's graveyard. Settlers began to take land around the village. Illinois Governor John Reynolds ordered the state militia to march on Saukenuk. Black Hawk and his band moved west across the Mississippi, but pledged to return.

In 1832, Black Hawk's band recrossed the Mississippi and sought Winnebago support. Contrary to the promises of Winnebago leaders, only a few Winnebagos joined. Black Hawk, his warriors, and

Black Hawk, a chief of the Sauk, defended the invasion of his homeland in 1832 in what has become known as the Black Hawk War.

their homeless families attacked frontier settlements in the area. In response, Governor Reynolds called out the militia again, assembling freshly recruited companies in the area. One of the new recruits was Abraham Lincoln, a young man at the time. (Lincoln's unit was later disbanded after its members took a vote over whether to fight Black Hawk. The vote was a tie. Lincoln later reenlisted but saw no fighting.)

Regular army troops were brought in to pursue Black Hawk's band, whose members had been forced to live on roots in the swamplands near the Mississippi. Several army and militia units caught Black Hawk and his people with their backs to the river. The Indians then hoisted a flag of truce. General Winfield Scott and other officers ignored the appeal for a truce and engaged in a one-sided slaughter that became known as the Battle of Black Ax.

Black Hawk, Neapope, and other survivors of the battle fled north to a Winnebago village, where they were betrayed for a bribe of twenty horses and one hundred dollars. Black Hawk was led away in chains by Jefferson Davis, who would later become president of the Confederate States of America. After several months in prison, Black Hawk was taken on a tour of several eastern cities; he met with President Andrew Jackson at the White House. Jackson gave Black Hawk a military uniform and a sword, but the aging chief was still angry. He told Jackson that he had made war to avenge injustice against his people. Behind Black Hawk's back, Jackson recognized Keokuk as principal chief of the Sauks and Foxes. The news came to Black Hawk and Keokuk as they stood together with army officers. Angry and frustrated, Black Hawk removed his breechcloth and slapped Keokuk across the face with it.

Eventually, Black Hawk settled on land governed by Keokuk, near what is now Iowaville on the Des Moines River. Shortly before his death, in 1838, Black Hawk acknowledged his defeat without lingering bitterness. He told a Fourth of July gathering near Fort Madison, "A few winters ago, I was fighting against you. I did wrong, perhaps, but that is past; it is buried; let it be forgotten. Rock River is a beautiful country. I liked my town, my cornfields, and the home of my people. I fought for it. It is now yours. Keep it as we did; it will produce you good crops."

— B. E. Johansen

SEE ALSO:
Keokuk; Sac and Fox; Winnebago.

SUGGESTED READINGS:
Beckhard, Arthur J. *Black Hawk.* New York: Julian Messner, 1957.
Black Hawk. *Life of Ma-ka-tai-me-she-kia-kiak, or Black Hawk, Dictated by Himself.* Boston, 1834.
Jackson, Donald, ed. *Black Hawk: An Autobiography.* Urbana: University of Illinois Press, 1964.
Waters, Frank. *Brave Are My People.* Santa Fe: Clear Light, 1992.

BLACK HILLS

West of the Missouri River in South Dakota, the flat expanse of plains begins to break up into rolling hills. A little farther west, tall grass, deep gullies, buttes, and the strange moonscape of the Badlands create fascinating vistas. Then, suddenly, rising against the sky, stand the Black Hills, an area rich in game, trees, water, sheltering valleys, minerals— and conflict—for more than one hundred years.

One of the Lakota names for this area is H'e Sapa, which describes the black ridges. Much scientific data points to Native occupation of the Hills as early as 1616 B.C.E., or at least by 896 B.C.E. Settlers, miners, and soldiers began arriving in the Hills in large numbers between 1874 and 1876. The 1851 Fort Laramie Treaty and every subsequent agreement between the Lakotas and the U.S. government stated that the Black Hills were to be protected from invaders and that the Powder River territory farther north would remain unceded— that is, retained by the Lakotas. The Fort Laramie Treaty of 1868, made after the Lakotas and their allies defeated the U.S. Army in the Powder River Wars, stated explicitly that the area retained by the Lakotas included the Black Hills. The treaty further stated that the army would help ensure that white people would stay out and that any future cession of land would require agreement from three-fourths of the adult male members of the tribe.

Soon after, however, gold was discovered, and in 1874, Lieutenant Colonel George Armstrong Custer made a highly publicized exploration and survey of the Black Hills. This opened the floodgates. But in 1875, the Lakotas refused President Ulysses Grant's offer of $6 million for the Hills.

In 1875, a great council of tribal leaders in the Hills discussed the U.S. government proposal that they sell the Black Hills. Their decision about selling was a resounding "no." The next year, Sitting Bull had his vision of many white soldiers falling into a Lakota camp, a vision that was fulfilled at the Battle at Greasy Grass.

In a letter dated November 9, 1875, Lieutenant General Phillip Sheridan informed General A. H. Terry, commander of the Department of the Dakota, that President Grant wanted miners in the hills left alone. This was a flagrant violation of Article XII of the 1868 Treaty. Within two years, the Lako-

The Black Hills are *H'e Sapa,* sacred land of the Sioux. American disrespect for H'e Sapa, particularly regarding mining practices, is a strong, contemporary motivation for the Sioux to reclaim it and care for it properly. It is a land of great contrasts. Here a wagon train is depicted crossing a portion of rolling grasslands.

tas lost all the land reserved for them in the treaty, including the 7.1 million acres (2.9 million hectares) of the Black Hills.

First, the Lakotas and their allies fought wars with the U.S. government over the Hills. Then, the battle moved to Congress and the courts. By the mid-1990s, the dispute over the Black Hills had become the longest-running case in federal court history.

The crux of the Lakotas' case is the 1877 taking of the Hills. In 1876, the U.S. government managed to get 241 Lakota men to sign an agreement to give up the Hills. This was far short of the 3,534 signatures for the three-fourths required by the treaty. Nonetheless, Congress ratified the "agreement" in 1877, taking the 7.1 million acres (2.9 million hectares) of the Black Hills. Even to get those 241 signatures required intimidation of the Lakotas. To get the signatures, the government destroyed the Lakotas' sustenance by exterminating the buffalo herds. The government then withheld rations, which they had contracted to provide in exchange for title to the land. This forced all of the Lakotas except Crazy Horse's people out of the Powder River Country and into the agencies. This forced cession is still called the "sign or starve" agreement.

Until the 1920s, the Lakotas had no recourse for their losses. But the first break in their efforts to regain their lands came in 1920, when Congress passed special legislation allowing them to bring suits in the Court of Claims, which they did three years later. These suits sought compensation for the misappropriation of their land. The Lakotas lost the case, however, and twenty years later the Supreme Court upheld the decision.

In 1946, Congress created the Indian Claims Commission (ICC) specifically to address monetary, and only monetary, compensation for Indian land losses. In 1954, four years after the Black Hills case came before it, the Claims Commission dismissed the suit, saying the Lakotas failed to prove their case. By then, the case had the designation Docket 74, a designation still used into the mid-1990s. The Court of Claims upheld the dismissal in 1956, but a year later the Court of Claims grant-

Devils Tower, a beautiful and mysterious-looking formation in the portion of the Black Hills that lies in northeastern Wyoming, as photographed at sunrise.

lion hectares) of the Black Hills taken from them. The court determined that the land was worth $17.1 million in 1877, plus 5 percent simple interest dating from 1877. By the time the court made this decision, however, mining corporations had extracted approximately $18 billion in gold, silver, uranium, and other natural resources from the Hills. With inflation and loss of minerals, the award amounted to less than one cent per acre.

The victory, such as it was, was short-lived. On June 25, 1976, the Court of Claims reversed the ICC decision. Ironically, this was exactly one hundred years to the day from the Battle at Greasy Grass and one year, short a day, after a reservation shoot-out between Oglalas and Federal Bureau of Investigation officials. Yet in that decision, the judges wrote, "A more ripe and rank case of dishonorable dealings will never in all probability be found in our history. . . ." The decision also said that President Grant had "breached" the government's obligation to keep trespassers out of the Black Hills and allowed the starving of the Sioux to get the agreement. The Supreme Court upheld the reversal.

ed a motion by the Lakotas to send the case back to the ICC because of an attorney error.

In 1960, the attorneys for the Lakotas divided the land claim into two cases. One involved lands outside western South Dakota (Docket 74B), and the other involved the Black Hills (Docket 74A).

After fourteen years, on February 15, 1974, the ICC voted four to one that the Lakotas deserved "just compensation" for 7.1 million acres (2.9 mil-

This decision, like all the court decisions and the prevailing attitudes in South Dakota, ignores the issue of freedom of religion and inherent rights of Native peoples—in this case, the Lakotas, for whom the Black Hills are sacred. David Getches, in *Federal Indian Law*, wrote that much of the Indian religious life does not include the existence of a church, periodic meetings, ritual, or identifiable dogma. Those who believe that doctrine and religious practices should be clearly defined by ancient writings or a central authority will have difficulty understanding and protecting Indian religion. "It is much easier for a non-Indian [to] comprehend worship in a church or synagogue," he wrote, "but not on a mountain top or with an eagle feather."

Others, such as *Time* magazine in the late 1980s, deplored any land return to Indians as dishonoring the bravery and virtues of the nineteenth-century pioneers. Gerald Clifford, an Oglala who coordinated the Black Hills Steering Committee from its inception in 1983, finds no difficulty in honoring both the pioneer spirit and the Lakotas. "We can continue to admire their [the pioneers'] virtues and contributions to building America. But it is time to hold up the virtues of the great Lakota men, women, and children who gave their lives in defense of their humanity, culture, religion, and way of life. We must [acknowledge] the greed, ignorance, and arrogance that set out and implemented the policy of manifest destiny."

The Lakotas' legal struggle did not end with the Court of Claims' reversal. Congressional and judicial skirmishes continued, along with changes in Lakota strategy and legal counsel. After representing the Lakotas for nearly thirty years and filing twenty-eight briefs, attorney Ralph Case resigned. He was under pressure from the tribes that wanted to pursue a return of the land, not monetary compensation.

A new law firm agreed to take on their case, but to the dismay of many Lakotas, the attorney who represented this firm continued the same strategy their previous attorney had pursued, despite repeated requests—and sometimes demands—from the tribes to pursue the return of the Hills. Although their attorney got the case reopened, he continued to operate under a cession strategy, in which the Lakota would receive money as compensation for land. Many felt that he should take the approach that the 1877 seizure of land was illegal because the agreement lacked the required signatures. This would mean that the U.S. government had unilaterally broken the 1868 treaty.

In 1977, the lawyer's contract with the tribes ended and was not renewed. The lawyer, however, continued to pursue the case. In 1978, the Indian Claims Commission awarded the Lakotas $44 million for the taking of land protected by the 1868 treaty. Congress passed legislation requiring the Court of Claims to hear the Black Hills case again, and the court affirmed the 1974 decision, awarding $103 million. Six years later, the Supreme Court awarded $106 million to the Lakotas for the Black Hills. The court refused, however, to allow the tribes' request that their lawyer be removed as counsel. The lawyer and his two coattorneys received $10.6 million out of the settlement for their twenty-three years of work.

The Lakotas, after long meetings on each reservation to consider the settlement, refused the money due them. Not a penny awarded under Docket 74A or 74B has ever reached the Lakotas. They did not—and do not—want it. They want their land. As Crazy Horse said the first time the U.S. government sought a cession of land from the Lakotas, "The earth upon which we walk is not for sale." A steady procession of Lakota leaders, from Red Cloud to those of the present day, have traveled to Washington, D.C., seeking the return of the Hills. In 1976, one of these leaders, Frank Kills Enemy, then eighty-two, an authority on treaties and Lakota history, testified before Congress, as he had done on many occasions. His grandfather had signed the 1868 Treaty, and Kills Enemy learned about it from him.

He explained, "We are a sovereign nation, but those who broke this treaty relationship sat in judgment on us both. . . . Only now are Indians beginning to demand what is rightfully theirs. We need to use international laws. If we use them, we will settle this claim if it takes another fifty years."

On August 24, 1970, a group of Lakotas, the Black Hills Sioux Teton Movement, protested at Mount Rushmore. In 1981, a group of Lakotas moved into the Black Hills and established Yellow Thunder Camp as a Lakota presence in the Hills. Despite constant threats of attack by park service rangers and U.S. marshals, the camp remained without armed confrontation for several years. One of many court actions connected to the camp refused permission for the Lakota tribes to establish a spiritual camp in the Hills, although

Although visitors have long been inspired by the natural beauty of the Black Hills, most non-Indians have had difficulty understanding the religious significance that the region holds for Native people.

a number of Christian churches have camps on public land in the Hills. In the first summer of Yellow Thunder's existence, the Oglala tribe established a second camp in the Wind Cave area in support of those at Yellow Thunder. In 1987, a coalition of Hills residents and Lakotas, called the Cowboy and Indian Alliance (the CIA) successfully prevented the Honeywell Corporation from establishing a munitions test site in an area now called Hell's Canyon, originally Thunder Eagle Canyon.

In the late 1980s, the Northern Cheyenne Tribe bought 560 acres (225 hectares) at Bear Butte and has another 120 acres (50 hectares) there held in trust by the U.S. government. The tribal council's cultural committee takes care of the area, and the Cheyennes always have access and protected privacy for their vision quests and other religious activities.

After another court setback in 1980, the Black Hills steering committee in 1981 began meetings with all Lakota tribes to draft legislation for the return of the Hills. It took twenty-nine meetings of the steering committee and tribes, as well as uncounted meetings within each tribe, to come to consensus on the bill. One observer termed this feat "a near miracle." On July 17, Senator Bill Bradley, a Democrat from New Jersey, introduced the Sioux Nation Black Hills Bill.

Bradley had two reasons for interest in this bill. As a basketball star with the New York Knicks, he had conducted a basketball camp at Pine Ridge. He saw the conditions on the reservation and made friends quickly, especially with his young players. Asked what they wanted most, the youngsters consistently replied, according to Bradley, "We want our Black Hills back." Bradley made up his mind that, given the opportunity, he would do what he could for his Oglala friends. As a senator, he could. His second reason: "I read American history, and I think about it."

The bill called for the return of 1.3 million acres (0.53 million hectares) of the 7.3 million acres (3 million hectares) in the Black Hills taken illegally by the U.S. government. All the land, except for Mount Rushmore, lies within the public domain of federal grasslands, forests, and parklands. The bill would not affect private and state land. Within that land, the legislation called for, among other things, establishment of a Sioux National Park, owned and operated by the Sioux Nation and open to all. The Sioux Nation would regulate hunting and fishing within the new reservation.

The bill also guaranteed that all rights of way, easements, and mineral and timber leases would remain in effect. The tribes would have first refusal to buy any private land and the chance to equal any private offer. Congress would set up a special account for the $180 million compensation already awarded for the other land taken in 1877. And the eight Sioux tribes with claims to the land would establish a national council to govern the newly acquired lands.

Back in his first action in the case, attorney Ralph Case had recognized that a suit for the land could be successful. He said he did not take that course, however, because "... the entire Black Hills country would rise up against the Sioux people." His assessment proved true. No amount of information about the bill could stop false allegations about the losses whites would suffer if the bill became law. By 1987, with untiring work by the steering committee, the tribes, Bradley, and Representative James Howard, also a New Jersey Democrat, the bill was making slow but steady progress after being reintroduced in the 100th Congress. Under the leadership of Democratic Senator Daniel Inouye of Hawaii, the Senate Select Committee on Indian Affairs held hearings. The bill gained more sponsors, who stressed the issue was a national one, not a local one as the South Dakota delegation claimed.

Then along came a millionaire, California business tycoon Phillip Stevens. Stevens had founded Ultrasystems, an Irvine, California, engineering company and defense contractor with ties to the Central Intelligence Agency. Instead of supporting the existing bill and its progress, he

used his money and public relations resources to push the tribes to seek an amendment to the Bradley Bill. The Stevens amendment called for $3 billion in reparations for lost land and minerals. With his money and contacts, Stevens assured the Lakotas he could get this version of the bill passed. This was despite concerns of people around the country over the severe national debt and cuts in even basic federal programs.

Stevens got enough support, especially from the Oglalas, to kill both the Bradley Bill and the Lakotas' consensus. He even began to claim Lakota heritage and got himself made a chief by a group of Sicangu Lakotas at Rosebud, causing an uproar in the traditional Lakota communities. Bradley withdrew his support, and Stevens never got his amendment any farther than just being introduced.

Even this disruption did not end the struggle. By the end of 1994, the Miniconjous of the Cheyenne River Reservation had new legislation ready to file in Congress. At Lakota Summit VI in July 1994, traditional and elected tribal leaders voted to seek legislation for the return of public lands, not only in the Black Hills but also in the Big Horn Mountains, the lands of the 1851 Treaty.

Edward Valandra, a Sicangu Lakota writer-activist, explained, "Much like non-white South Africa's presence [before democratic elections] the Lakota presence [in the Hills] is unrelenting.... Unfortunately, for whites ... in South Dakota to deny the Lakota their homeland in reality denies the one quality they desire—a sense of place."

After all, no one forgets her or his heart, and to the Sioux, the H'e Sapa is the heart of everything that is.

— C. Hamilton

SEE ALSO:
Crazy Horse; Custer, George Armstrong; Fort Laramie Treaty of 1851; Fort Laramie Treaty of 1868; Manifest Destiny; Siouan Nations; Sitting Bull.

BLACK INDIANS

SEE African-Americans; Florida; Florida, Indians of; Georgia; Seminole.

BLACK KETTLE (1803–1868)

Black Kettle (Mo-ke-ta-va-ta) was one of the chiefs of the southern Cheyenne in the mid-1800s. After the famous Cheyenne Roman Nose was killed, Black Kettle became the principal chief of the southern Cheyenne.

Much controversy has swirled around Black Kettle and his association with Euro-Americans. In many non-Indian historical accounts, he has often been described as a bloodthirsty warrior who led warriors in actions that took many settlers' lives. In other accounts, he is described primarily as an advocate of peace and as an advocate for the Cheyenne entering into treaties with Euro-Americans. Black Kettle was almost certainly involved in some attacks on non-Indians, but he may have shifted his response to whites when he realized that they existed in numbers that made victory impossible.

Throughout his life, Black Kettle was involved in a number of incidents in which conflicting accounts exist of what actually happened. The first of these events took place in 1864. Black Kettle and the principal chief of the Arapaho, Left Hand, met with Colorado Governor John Evans in Denver. At the time of the meeting, a state of emergency existed among settlers and soldiers in Colorado. The Cheyenne and Arapaho were actively resisting westward expansion into their territory, but the Arapaho had lost almost all of their traditional hunting areas. They responded to this loss by attacking settlers' wagon trains, stagecoaches, and farms. Militia and army units attacked Indian bands, but the bands they could find were usually peaceful groups that did not attempt to avoid the military. Men, women, and children on both sides were killed in confrontations between Natives and non-Natives.

In modern accounts, it is not clear what Black Kettle and Left Hand expected to come from their meeting with Governor Evans, although they appear to have been seeking a peace treaty. Accounts do make it clear that the meeting was not a peaceful one, however. The governor grilled the two chiefs with questions about Indian atrocities and finally told them that it was not in his power to make a peace treaty and that they should deal with the military commander in the district, Colonel John M.

Chivington. Despite Evans's claims not to have any knowledge or authority in dealings with Black Kettle and Left Hand, however, he probably knew that Chivington was under orders from his commander, General S. R. Curtis, to attack the Cheyenne and Arapaho anywhere he found them. Curtis had told Chivington that there might be peace in the future, but in the meantime, the Indians were to be "chastised." (The army policy at that time was that Indians should be "chastised"— or punished—before they were brought into treaty agreements so that they could first understand the power of the U.S. Army. The use of a term that means "punished" also carries with it the understanding that the Indians were "guilty" of something to be punished for.)

There are accounts that, in collusion with other army officers, Chivington urged Black Kettle and his band to camp at Sand Creek, near Fort Lyon. Black Kettle had been told that his band would be safe from attack at the Sand Creek site. But Colonel Chivington had secretly made plans to attack Black Kettle's band and did so on the morning of November 29, 1864. What happened next became the subject of many accounts and inquiries, and later, both military and Congressional panels investigated the attack. One of the many accounts came from George Bent, a half-breed trader who was in Black Kettle's camp when the attack was launched. Bent said that Black Kettle raised a large American flag to indicate that the camp was friendly. But the flag was ignored, and a wholesale slaughter of the Indians followed. By different accounts, between three hundred and six hundred Indians were killed. The military account stated that half the dead were warriors and the rest were women and children caught in the gunfire. Indian accounts state that as few as sixty of the dead were men. Other accounts report horrible mutilations of women and children by the soldiers. Only two women and five children were taken prisoner.

Black Kettle escaped early in the battle, but not all of his family members were so fortunate. His brother, White Antelope, was killed during the battle.

Between 1864 and 1867, Black Kettle resumed his attacks on non-Indians. Even though a treaty was signed at Medicine Creek Lodge in late 1867, hostilities still continued.

In the fall of 1868, Black Kettle and his band moved to a camp on the Washita River in Oklahoma. General Philip H. Sheridan ordered Lt. Colonel George Armstrong Custer to attack the Indians camped along the Washita. Early on the morning of November 27, 1868, almost four years to the day after the massacre at Sand Creek, Black Kettle's camp was again attacked by the U.S. military. The soldiers killed 103 Native people; many of the dead were again women and children. This time, Black Kettle would also be counted among the dead.

Chief Black Kettle is most often remembered in connection with Sand Creek and Washita. He was a chief who resisted the invasion of his land and the domination of his people by soldiers and settlers. Both he and his people paid a great price for their resistance.

— T. Colonnese

Black Kettle, who fiercely resisted U.S. expansion into Indian lands, also worked tirelessly for peace. In 1864, he met with members of a Denver peace delegation—just weeks before the massacre of Cheyennes and Arapahos by army troops at Sand Creek.

SEE ALSO:
Custer, George Armstrong; Sand Creek Massacre; Washita, Battle of the.

BLACKFEET

The Blackfeet Nation has historically consisted of three allied tribes, the northern Piegan (Pikuni), the Blood (Kainah), and the Siksika (literally "black foot"). The name Siksika is also used for the entire Blackfeet Nation.

The Blackfeet live on both sides of the U.S.-Canadian border in Montana and Alberta. All three tribes speak a common language—belonging to the Algonquian language family—and share the same customs, culture, and family kinships. The Blackfeet Reservation, located in northern Montana, comprises 1.5 million acres (0.6 million hectares) of land just to the east of Glacier National Park and just south of the Canadian border. There are also three Canadian reserves for the Blackfeet in the province of Alberta.

Historically, the tribes that make up today's Blackfeet Nation lived in an area stretching from Saskatchewan and Alberta in Canada to Montana and Idaho in the United States. According to their oral traditions, they once lived around the Great Lakes, later moving to the Great Plains region. There, they hunted buffalo, which supplied much of their food and clothing and provided hides for their tipis. The traditional religion includes secret

A Blackfeet tribal member in Glacier National Park, in Montana.

Christian religion among the Blackfeet is Catholicism.

Until the mid-1800s, the Blackfeet controlled an area twice the size of present-day New England and kept fur trappers and traders out of their part of the Rockies. But early in the century, the power of the Blackfeet began to wane. In 1836, a smallpox epidemic reduced the Blackfeet population. In 1859, the first mission school, called Saint Peters, was opened for the tribe in Choteau, Montana. In 1883, another mission school was started in Robare, Montana. The Blackfeet continued to skirmish with their traditional enemies, the Assiniboine, Cree, Crow, Flathead, Kalispel (Pend d'Oreille), and Kutenai, until 1887. With the opening of mission schools, however, traditional Blackfeet culture began to be undermined.

In exchange for land, the United States made a series of treaties with the Blackfeet, promising education, food, health care, money, peace, and protection. Most of these commitments were not kept by the United States. The Blackfeet land area continued to shrink even after the end of the great treaty-making period in 1871.

By the early 1880s, the buffalo were hunted almost to extinction. Therefore, the Blackfeet became dependent on the government for food, shelter, and supplies. In the fall of 1883, the promised supplies did not arrive, and over six hundred Montana Piegan alone starved and froze to death. That winter was called "starvation winter."

The great American western artist Charles Russell painted many Blackfeet scenes around the turn of the twentieth century. Russell's painting documented a way of life that was quickly changing.

In 1907, an amendment to the Dawes Allotment of 1887 provided each member of an Indian tribe 320 acres (130 hectares) of land. The rest of

societies and the Sun Dance. Today, while this religion is still practiced, many Blackfeet are Christians.

European contact occurred in the 1700s as fur traders ranged west. Guns and horses were obtained from the traders and other tribes and quickly put to use for buffalo hunting and war. The Blackfeet were considered by Europeans and neighboring tribes to be one of the most powerful of the northwestern tribes. They were often at war with the Gros Ventre, the Assiniboine, and the Shoshone, among others.

Missionaries arrived in the Blackfeet area in the early 1800s. The missionaries did not meet with great success early on. But today, the main

the Indian land was sold to homesteaders by the U.S. government for a profit. By 1920, disease, war, and starvation had reduced the Blackfeet population to only two thousand people. The tribe did not really begin to recover until the Indian Reorganization Act of 1934, when the U.S. government's Indian policy became more accepting toward Indian self-determination. In 1935, the Blackfeet Tribal Business Council was formed to handle tribal business ventures and assist in efforts at tribal self-determination. Browning, Montana, became the current center of tribal business and government. In 1935, the tribe began to prosper and now has over fourteen thousand members. The tribe continues to plan and work toward improving the conditions of its people.

North American Indian Days is celebrated in Browning, Montana, for four days during the second week in July on the Blackfeet Tribal Fairgrounds. This is one of the largest Plains Indian celebrations drawing together Native people from throughout North America.

— J. D. Berry

SEE ALSO:
Dawes Commission; General Allotment Act.

SUGGESTED READINGS:
Hirschfelder, Arlene, and Martha Kreipe de Montaña. *The Native American Almanac.* New York: Prentice Hall, 1993.

Nabokov, Peter, ed. *Native American Testimony, A Chronicle of Indian-White Relations from Prophecy to the Present.* New York: Viking Penguin, 1991.

Utley, Robert M. *The Indian Frontier of the American West, 1846–1890.* Albuquerque: University of New Mexico Press, 1983.

BLAESER, KIMBERLY M. (1955–)

Kimberly M. Blaeser, of mixed Anishinabe (Ojibwe) and German ancestry, is one the most active and versatile of Native literary writers. She is also a skilled orator and one of the leading scholars of Native American literary criticism. A member of the Minnesota Chippewa Tribe, Blaeser grew up on White Earth Reservation in Minnesota. She received her doctorate in English at the University of Notre Dame in Indiana. She currently teaches comparative literature at the University of Wisconsin-Milwaukee.

Kimberly Blaeser, of the Minnesota Chippewa Tribe, grew up on White Earth Reservation. Her first book of poetry, *Trailing You*, won the 1993 Diane Decorah Memorial Poetry Award.

Blaeser's poetry has appeared widely in many publications, such as *Loonfeather* and *Akwe:kon Journal*, and in anthologies such as *Durable Breath* (Salmon Run Press, 1994), *Returning the Gift* (University of Arizona Press, 1994), and *The Colour of Resistance* (Sister Vision Press, 1994). Her first book of poetry, *Trailing You* (Greenfield Review Press, 1994), won the 1993 Diane Decorah Memorial Poetry Award from fellow Native American poets in the Native Writers' Circle of the Americas. Another of her books, *Gerald Vizenor: Writing in the Oral Tradition*, is an outgrowth of her doctoral dissertation on the literary work of fellow Anishinabe writer Gerald Vizenor. It is being published by the University of Oklahoma Press. Blaeser has also written numerous literary analyses of Native American literature.

Blaeser's short stories have appeared in literary quarterlies such as *Calalloo* (Johns Hopkins University Press) and in anthologies such as *Earth Song, Sky Spirit* (Doubleday, 1993). Blaeser was a keynote speaker at the 1995 Returning the Gift conference of Native literary writers in Green Bay, Wisconsin, and at the 1992 Returning the Gift conference at the University of Oklahoma. An extract of her 1992 speech may be found in the Spring 1993 issue of *Akwe:kon Journal*, published by the American Indian Program of Cornell University.

SEE ALSO:
Returning the Gift.

BLUE LAKE

Blue Lake, near Mt. Wheeler in northeastern New Mexico, is the sacred lake of Taos Pueblo. In 1970, Blue Lake, and forty-eight thousand acres (twenty thousand hectares) of surrounding land, became the first land returned to Indian people by the U.S. government for traditional Indian religious purposes. The restoration of Blue Lake ended a sixty-four-year struggle by the people of Taos Pueblo to regain their sacred lake.

The struggle began in 1906 when Blue Lake, along with 130,000 surrounding acres (50,000 hectares), was declared a public forest reserve and placed under the administration of the United States Forest Service by President Theodore Roosevelt. Blue Lake became a part of the Carson National Forest in 1908. Taos Pueblo protested that the Forest Service was enacting land-use policies that interfered with its religious observances, that non-Indians were being granted recreational permits at the lake, and that cattle ranchers were being granted ten-year grazing permits.

In 1912, and again in 1916, Taos Pueblo attempted unsuccessfully to have Blue Lake declared an executive order reservation by the secretary of the interior. Over the years, as many as ten different pieces of legislation were introduced into Congress to resolve the dispute, but all failed to gain final approval. In 1951, Taos Pueblo argued its case before the Indian Claims Commission. Sixteen years later, the commission ruled in favor of Taos Pueblo but was authorized only to compensate for monetary losses. This ruling was unsatisfactory to Taos Pueblo. Finally, in 1970, Congress passed, and President Richard Nixon signed, legislation restoring title to Blue Lake to Taos Pueblo.

SEE ALSO:
Pueblo; Taos Pueblo.

BOARDING SCHOOLS

Since the colonial era, Europeans and European-Americans have used education in an attempt to extinguish the cultures of the indigenous peoples of the Americas. Boarding schools were widely used from early in the period of Spanish and British colonization in North America. The British sent many Native young people to the "Indian College" at Williamsburg, Virginia, before the American Revolution. Boarding schools have also been widely used in Canada up to recent times.

The education of Native American children has been a policy of the U.S. government since the earliest days of the republic. Henry Knox, the first secretary of war, suggested to President George Washington in 1789 that the new federal government pursue a policy of education of the American Indians. Many subsequent treaties signed with Indian nations contained stipulations that the U.S. government would provide education for the children.

This photo, taken around 1880, shows a group of Omaha Indians in uniforms at Carlisle Indian School. From colonial times, boarding schools were used to "civilize" Indian children and lead them away from their Native cultures.

In the years following, the makeup of a "good" education for Native Americans would continue as a matter of enormous controversy. Not only have educational policies shifted over time with the changes in the philosophy of education, but politics and self-interest have played a large role in the educational practices applied to Native American children by others.

The earliest philosophy behind the schooling of Native American children was to promote their acculturation, or blending, into the dominant American society. This process was often referred to as "civilizing the Indians." (In the view of many Native people, this effort to "blend" Native peoples into dominant society is a form of cultural genocide.) The first schools were often attached to colleges, while others were mission schools, established by various church missions with money received from U.S. government contracts. Mission-based education predominated for approximately ninety years with the establishment of both day schools and boarding schools throughout the United States.

In the late 1800s, the federal government began founding its own day schools, reservation boarding schools, and off-reservation boarding schools. These schools were administered by the federal government through the Bureau of Indian Affairs. The first off-reservation, government-run boarding school was opened in Carlisle, Pennsylvania, at an abandoned army installation on November 1, 1879. Carlisle Indian School, which was run by Captain R. H. Pratt, was soon followed by many others. The curricula at the boarding schools often focused on industrial or manual labor training, as opposed to academic preparation. The boarding schools employed strict military discipline and were often compared to reform schools. Many boarding schools also used the "outing system" or outplacement service. With this system, an older Indian student would be placed with a local Anglo-American family in order to live and work for a period of time. The thought was that the removal of an Indian child from his or her home, to be totally immersed in another culture, was a "civilizing" influence upon that student. The system was designed to mold him or her into a model U.S. citizen. It was also designed to cause the student to cease being an Indian, culturally, religiously, and linguistically.

The boarding school system proved to be a barbaric institution that had a traumatic effect on the students and their families. In the late nineteenth century, some of these students wrote about their experiences. They described the horror of being taken away from their families and the shock of being abruptly inserted into a strange environment. Their clothing was removed and discarded, and their hair was cut—in many Native cultures, a practice performed only as a sign of mourning. They were spoken to in a strange language (English) and were punished if they tried to speak their own Native language. Discipline was harsh, and many children were beaten or locked in a closet for disobeying rules they did not understand. The children were used as laborers at the schools, in the laundries, cafeterias, vegetable gardens, and other areas requiring labor, and they were also used as laborers in the white homes in the outing system. The children were kept away from their homes and loved ones for many years without any communication. When they finally did return home, they found that they were often estranged from their own families.

In some ways, the boarding schools were effective, but in a way that devastated Native culture. They produced students who could read and write English and who were trained for low-wage jobs in the dominant society. Unfortunately, this meant that the students had become unfit to take their places in their own communities, which contributed to a breakdown in the Native American societal structure. The story of the boarding school students is one of loss: loss of language, loss of lifestyle, loss of family, loss of community. Written accounts of the period detail the feelings of

Girls receiving instruction in shorthand at Haskell Institute in 1910.

A class in blacksmithing at Forest Grove School, Oregon, 1882.

anguish those students had. They did not feel that they had a place in their own society, nor in Anglo-American society. Some students, however, found ways of resisting the forced loss of their culture. Some became runaways. Others resisted by continuing to speak their Native languages in secret and continuing their own ceremonies out of the watchful eyes of the boarding school administrators.

Shortly after the turn of the century, the drawbacks of the boarding schools were recognized and their numbers began to decline. Half of the original number were closed within the next fifteen years. In more recent years, the few remaining boarding schools have been recommended only for students who come from disrupted families or whose homes are so physically remote that education cannot be obtained in any other way. Usually, only older children are sent to boarding schools.

There appears to be little doubt that the use of off-reservation government boarding schools played a large role in the loss of Native American language and cultural identity for some of the Native people in the United States. Another critical effect, however, was to create a network of boarding-school-educated Native people who were familiar enough with the U.S. government and political affairs to begin successful pan-Indian reform movements in the first half of the twentieth century. In the twentieth century, intertribal friendships, marriages, and networking have made Native people better able to join together in resisting efforts to extinguish their cultures.

—M. A. Stout

SEE ALSO:

Carlisle Indian School; Hampton Institute; Missions for Indians, Christian.

SUGGESTED READINGS:

Adams, David Wallace. *Education for Extinction: American Indians and the Boarding School Experience, 1875–1928.* Lawrence: University Press of Kansas, 1995.

Hoxie, Frederick E. *A Final Promise: The Campaign to Assimilate the Indians, 1880–1920.* Lincoln: University of Nebraska Press, 1984.

Lindsey, Donel F. *Indians at Hampton Institute, 1877–1923.* Urbana: University of Illinois Press, 1995.

Lomawaima, K. Tsianiana. *They Called It Prairie Light: The Story of Chilocco Indian School.* Lincoln: University of Nebraska Press, 1994.

Trennert, Robert A. *The Phoenix Indian School.* Norman: University of Oklahoma Press, 1988.

BOLDT, GEORGE HUGO (1903–)

On February 12, 1974, U.S. District Court Judge George Boldt ruled that Native people living in the Puget Sound area of Washington state were entitled to catch as many as half the fish returning to off-reservation spawning sites that had been the "usual and accustomed places" when treaties were signed in the 1850s. The case became an object of major controversy between Natives and non-Indian commercial and sports fishers.

Boldt (who was himself not an Indian) had put three years into the case. He used two hundred pages to interpret one sentence of a treaty, in what some legal scholars call the most carefully researched and thoroughly analyzed opinion ever handed down in an Indian fishing-rights case.

The nucleus of Boldt's decision had to do with nineteenth-century dictionaries' definitions of *in common with*. Boldt said the phrase meant "to be shared equally." The Ninth Circuit Court of Appeals upheld Boldt's ruling, and the U.S. Supreme Court twice let the ruling stand by refusing to hear further appeals.

In 1974, U.S. District Court Judge George Boldt ruled in favor of Native fishermen on Puget Sound in the state of Washington, setting off a nationwide debate about Indian treaty rights.

Judge Boldt's ruling had a profound effect not only on who would be allowed to catch salmon in Puget Sound but on relations between Indians and non-Indians generally. A widely held view among whites was that the ruling gave an unfair advantage to Indians. Non-Indians in the state of Washington had long regarded the salmon harvest as virtually their own. Suddenly, they faced the prospect of large reductions in their catch, which might force them out of the fishing industry. Rumors circulated about the sanity of Judge Boldt, who had been born in 1903. It was said that he had taken bribes of free fish and had an Indian mistress, neither of which was true. Bumper stickers proclaimed "Can Judge Boldt," and he was hanged in effigy. Hostility grew to the point that some non-Indian fishers formed "convoys" with their boats and rammed U.S. Coast Guard vessels that had been dispatched to enforce Boldt's ruling. One coastguardsman was shot. Indians armed their fishing camps after enduring attacks on themselves and their equipment.

Lost in the fray were a number of small, landless, western Washington tribes that were not recognized by the federal government and therefore not entitled to participate in the federally mandated solution. A few such tribes, such as the Upper Skagit and Sauk-Suiattle, were recognized after the Boldt decision. A number of others remained in legal limbo, with no fishing rights under federal law.

While the commercial interests raged, the Indians of the Puget Sound area were catching nothing close to the 50 percent allowed by the Boldt ruling. Instead—depending on who did the counting, the Indians or the state—Indians caught between 7 and 8 percent in 1974, between 11 and 12 percent in 1975, between 13 and 25 percent in 1976, and 17 percent in 1977.

SEE ALSO:
Fishing Rights; Lummi; Washington State.

BONNIN, GERTRUDE (1876–1938)

Gertrude Bonnin (Yankton Dakota) provided a written view of Sioux life at the juncture of two eras. Born in the same year as the Battle of the Little Bighorn, she died on the eve of World War II.

Gertrude Bonnin, a Yankton Dakota, at a meeting of the National Women's Party in Washington, D.C., in February 1921. Under the pen name Zitkala-sa, Bonnin investigated Indian land fraud in Oklahoma that followed the discovery of oil.

Although Bonnin distrusted most non-Indians, she sought a formal education against her mother's wishes and attended the Boston Conservatory of Music, where she became an accomplished violinist. Later, Bonnin's articles and poetry were published in large-circulation magazines. One of her books was autobiographical: *American Indian Stories* (1921), which described her changing perceptions of the Euro-American world and her gradual acceptance of Christianity. Bonnin also authored *Old Indian Legends* (1901).

With Charles Eastman, Bonnin was cofounder of the Society of American Indians, a pan-Indian advocacy organization active from 1911 to the mid-1920s. She taught for a time at Carlisle Indian School. Under the pen name Zitkala-sa, Bonnin investigated the swindling of Indians in Oklahoma by white settlers who swarmed the area after the discovery of oil. She also advised the government's Meriam Commission in the late 1920s. Bonnin remained active in Indian affairs until her death.

SEE ALSO:
Eastman, Charles A.; Siouan Nations; Standing Bear, Luther.

BOONE, DANIEL (1734–1820)

Daniel Boone was one of the late eighteenth century's better-known Anglo-American colonizers. Boone was born in Bucks County, Pennsylvania. He was a grandson of George Boone, a Quaker who had arrived in Pennsylvania in 1717 with his wife and eleven children. George Boone's son Squire married Sarah Morgan, who gave birth to Daniel in 1734. Daniel moved with his family to Holman's Ford in North Carolina in 1748.

Daniel Boone's life has become a symbol to Native Americans of the disregard of English colonists for the rights of indigenous peoples in North America. In the Proclamation of 1763, the English king specifically forbade the colonists from crossing the Appalachian Mountains. Daniel Boone, and many other colonists, simply ignored the law.

An eighteenth-century encyclopedia said that Boone could read and write, but "beyond that all he knew related to the fields, the woods, the net, the rifle, and hunting. He was a hunter born, and he loved the solitude of the forest. Strong, brave, lithe [agile], inured [accustomed] to hardship and privation, he sought out the hiding places of panther, bear, and wolf." The same book said that Boone's tracking skills were "the match of any Indian."

Boone married Rebecca Bryan about 1755 in North Carolina but soon became restless as settlement closed in around his home there. In 1769, Boone and six others left North Carolina to strike out into the area that would become Kentucky. Boone served for a time in Lord Dunsmore's War and later constructed a fort on the Kentucky River, naming it Boonesborough. Boone guided his wife and about thirty others from North Carolina to Boonesborough, where a full-fledged community was then established.

Some time later, Boone was leading about thirty men in search of a supply of salt at a place called Salt Licks, about 100 miles (160 kilometers) north of Boonesborough, when the party was taken prisoner by Indian warriors led by two Frenchmen. All the prisoners except Boone were ransomed. Boone himself was taken to Chillicothe in present-day Ohio, where he was adopted by Shawnee Chief Blackfish. Boone was initiated by Blackfish in a painful ritual that involved the plucking out of all his hair except for a tuft on the forehead. Having been adopted, Boone learned that Blackfish was planning to march on Boonesborough. In 1778, Boone resolved to escape Blackfish's people, and he did so with 450 Indians chasing him.

Boone is said to have covered the 160 miles (260 kilometers) to Boonesborough in four days on foot, eating only one meal, to find that his wife and children had given him up for dead and returned to North Carolina. The Indians under Blackfish did attack the fort but were driven away. Boone journeyed to North Carolina to join his family and returned with them to Kentucky in 1780. That same year, Boone's brother Squire was killed by Indians, whom Daniel narrowly escaped. Two years later, in another battle near his home, one of Boone's two surviving sons was killed by Indians. The other was severely wounded.

In 1792, Kentucky became a state. When the state was surveyed, Boone's land title was disputed. He lost the case in court and moved to a new settlement at Point Pleasant in Ohio. In 1795, Boone

Here, as in popular myth, Anglo-American colonist Daniel Boone is portrayed as a hero. To Native Americans, his life is a symbol of Euro-American disregard for the rights of the indigenous peoples of North America.

moved to present-day Missouri, which was under Spanish rule at the time. He obtained a grant to 8,000 acres (3,250 hectares) but lost his land title after France took control of the area and then sold it to the United States as part of the Louisiana Purchase in 1803. Boone appealed to Congress, which granted him 850 acres (350 hectares), on which he lived until his death during a hunting expedition.

SEE ALSO:
Kentucky; Missouri; Ohio; Shawnee.

BOSQUE REDONDO

Bosque Redondo was a concentration camp operated by the United States on the Pecos River at Fort Sumner in east-central New Mexico. By March 1863, four hundred Mescalero Apaches had been interned there by the U.S. Army. The following year, more than eight thousand Navajos were forced to march to Fort Sumner, a trip of nearly 400 miles (650 kilometers) from their homeland, a march known as "the Long Walk."

Brigadier General James Carleton, who was commander of the U.S. Army in New Mexico Territory, conceived the idea of concentrating Mescaleros and Navajos on the arid high plains of eastern New Mexico. He wanted to establish U.S. authority over the region. Mescaleros and Navajos had resisted the intrusion of the United States into their lives, and the government had responded with military action. Army troops under the command of Colonel Kit Carson burned Navajo crops, cut down their orchards, killed their sheep and horses, and starved the entire nation into surrender. Many Navajos, at least one thousand and possibly several thousand, fled the Navajo homeland to hide in remote canyons to the north and west. Most of the Navajo population, however, was marched all the way across New Mexico to Bosque Redondo; many died. Once there, General Carleton intended that the Mescaleros and Navajos be taught agriculture and Christianity and then, after a few years, that they be relocated to reservations, probably in present-day Oklahoma.

From the outset, the resources of Bosque Redondo proved far too slight for so large a population. When the Navajos came, the Mescaleros were already cultivating the best land for agriculture along the river. With the arrival of the Navajos, the Mescaleros were forced to restrict their cultivation to a small corner of the tract. Soon forty Mescaleros fled Bosque Redondo. The next year, they all left.

Serious problems abounded. The Navajos were issued shovels and forced to dig an irrigation ditch seven miles (eleven kilometers) long. They planted six thousand acres (twenty-five hundred hectares) of corn, beans, wheat, and pumpkins, but caterpillars destroyed nearly the entire crop. The army issued meager rations of bacon, flour, and coffee to them, but the Navajos had no idea what to do with the bitter coffee beans. They tried chewing them. They boiled them for hours trying to make them soft enough to eat.

Flour was equally foreign. The Navajos were provided with no shelter, except for a few Indians, who were given old army tents. Most Navajo families slept huddled together in shallow pits, protected only by a thin covering of boughs. There were no trees suitable for use in construction within twenty-five miles (forty kilometers) of the camp, and the few cottonwoods along the river were soon cut down. Then they had to travel ten to twenty miles (fifteen to thirty kilometers) to find wood for fuel. The alkaline water made them sick.

To make matters worse, the army and the Bureau of Indian Affairs were jealous of each other's authority and resentful of what each regarded as an intrusion into its sphere by the other branch of the government. No one had anticipated the monumental problems of trying to guard and feed such a large population. Congress appropriated $100,000 for the Navajos in 1864, but graft at every stage at which the money was handled reduced

the amount that reached the Navajos to about $30,000 worth of shoddy goods. Blankets issued to them were of such poor quality that the Navajos had to untwist the threads and try to weave them back together.

Americans tried to impose their culture in various ways. Priests arrived from Santa Fe and began to operate a school. The army, without attempting to understand the organization of the Navajos into bands, each with its own leaders, decided to create its own government for the nation. It chose twelve prominent Navajos and divided the entire nation into twelve units, each under the jurisdiction of one of the army-created leaders, an arrangement that the United States would continue to impose on Navajos for fifty years.

In 1865 and 1866, the crops failed again, and Comanches raided their livestock. The Navajos suffered miserably, especially during the winters, and nearly a thousand of them left the camp. Hundreds of others had died. Bosque Redondo became the subject of government investigations.

But the issue was not the treatment of the Navajos, it was money. Bosque Redondo had cost the U.S. Army more than one million dollars just for the first eighteen months—and that was not counting congressional appropriations. In September 1866, General Carleton was relieved of command, and three months later, the Department of the Interior was placed in charge.

By 1867, conditions had become so bad that the Navajos refused to plant any crops. The next winter, several hundred more left the camp, and the next spring, they were all demanding to leave.

Admitting failure, especially regarding mounting expenses that it no longer wanted to pay, in May 1868, the army sent special commissioners to Bosque Redondo, who intended to negotiate a treaty for the removal of the nation to present-day Oklahoma.

The Navajo leaders talked them out of it and negotiated a return to their homeland, agreeing to recognize the authority of the United States in the Southwest in return for the recognition of their right to live in peace in their homeland. The treaty was signed on June 1, 1868, and a few weeks later, the Navajos began returning to their homes.

— D. L. Birchfield

SEE ALSO:
Long Walk, Navajo; Mescalero Apache; Navajo; Navajo Reservation.

BOSTON TEA PARTY

SEE Mohawk; Revere, Paul.

BOUDINOT, ELIAS (c. 1803–1839)

Elias Boudinot (Cherokee) was an outspoken editor of the *Cherokee Phoenix* and an early opponent of the removal policy that eventually led to the Trail of Tears. He was born near Rome, Georgia, as Buck Watie. In 1818, he took the name of his benefactor, philanthropist Elias Boudinot. He also was known as Galagina (meaning "Mule Deer") and Stag Watie.

Boudinot was a son of David Uwati and a mixed-blood Cherokee woman named Susannah Reese. As a young boy, he studied at the Moravian school in Salem, North Carolina. From 1818 to 1822, he attended the Cornwall Foreign Mission School in Cornwall, Connecticut, through a scholarship provided by Elias Boudinot of New Jersey. Young Boudinot met and fell in love with a local white girl, Harriet Ruggles Gold, while at the Cornwall school. Their marriage was violently opposed by most of the town, and Harriet's own brother burned the couple in effigy. However, Harriet remained firm in her decision to marry the man she loved.

In December 1822, Boudinot returned to his homeland, where he served as clerk of the Cherokee National Council. In 1827, the council authorized a national newspaper. On February 21, 1828, Boudinot's name appeared as the first editor of the weekly *Cherokee Phoenix*, published in Sequoyah's newly fashioned syllabary and English. The associate editor was Stephen Foreman. As editor, Boudinot took a strong position against removal. In 1831, he traveled through the North to raise funds to continue publishing the *Phoenix*. During this time, he wrote the first novel published in Cherokee, titled *Poor Sarah, or the Indian Woman*.

Boudinot also collaborated with Stephen Foreman and Samuel Worcester on a translation of the Bible into Cherokee. In September 1833, he resigned as editor of the *Cherokee Phoenix*.

Some months earlier, Boudinot had reversed his opposition to removal. Georgia officials had begun surveying Cherokee lands in 1832. Members of the Treaty Party—including Boudinot, his brother Stand Watie, Major Ridge, and John Ridge—felt that removal was becoming unavoidable.

Fearing annihilation of the Cherokee if they resisted, Boudinot and other members of the Treaty Party advised that the best possible terms for removal should be secured. John Ross and his faction decided to oppose removal through the courts. Boudinot, John Ridge, and several others journeyed to Washington, D.C., in 1835 to negotiate removal, though their efforts were not officially sanctioned by the Cherokee government. On December 29, 1835, Boudinot and nineteen other Cherokees signed the Treaty of New Echota, giving up Cherokee lands. On May 23, 1836, the controversial treaty was ratified by a one-vote margin in the U.S. Senate. This treaty led to the Cherokee Trail of Tears, during which more than 20 percent of the tribe died.

Upon arriving in Indian Territory (now Oklahoma) in late 1837, Boudinot settled at Park Hill. On June 22, 1839, Boudinot was killed by several Cherokee traditionalists who invoked the Law of Blood for Boudinot's unsanctioned sale of Cherokee lands.

Boudinot's first wife, Harriet, had died in 1830, leaving him with six children. Boudinot's second wife, Delight Sargent Boudinot, took the children to the East for their education. Boudinot's most famous son, Elias Cornelius Boudinot, attended school in Vermont. He studied civil engineering and later became a leader among the Western Cherokee. Along with his uncle, Stand Watie, Elias Cornelius sided with the Confederacy during the Civil War. Attending as a delegate from the Cherokee Nation, he served as a member of the Confederate Congress in Richmond, Virginia.

SEE ALSO:
Cherokee Phoenix; Removal Act, Indian; Ross, John; Trail of Tears; Watie, Stand.

BOZEMAN TRAIL AND THE BATTLE OF A HUNDRED SLAIN

The Bozeman Trail to the Montana gold mines ran through the Powder River Country, which was the heart of Lakota, Arapaho, and Cheyenne lands. The Powder River Country lay between what is now the Platte, Yellowstone, and Upper Missouri Rivers and the Rocky Mountains. From 1865 to 1868, the Trail caused trouble between the Lakotas and non-Native settlers, immigrants, and miners, as well as the U.S. Army. After the Civil War ended, waves of these newcomers poured westward into the Powder River Country.

Even before the end of the war, however, steamboats loaded with Oregon immigrants, Mormons, trappers, and hunters brought foreign substances to the area. These included alcohol and diseases such as measles, smallpox, and cholera. The Native people had no resistance to these nor any treatment for them. For example, smallpox reduced one Mandan group of 1,600 to 150 sickly people. In addition to bringing diseases, settlers and soldiers also destroyed the hunting grounds, timber tracts, buffalo herds, and grasslands needed for feeding the tribes' horses.

The U.S. government wanted the Bozeman Trail to link the Oregon Trail northward into the Montana gold fields. The trails joined at Fort Laramie in southeastern Wyoming, with the Bozeman extending north and west. Forts Philip Kearny and C. F. Smith were supposed to protect travelers on the trail to Bozeman and to Virginia City in what is now Montana. The tribal people wanted no further encroachment on or travel through their lands, as promised in the Treaty of 1851. For their part, whites were equally determined to open up the region to settlement and gold mining. To complicate matters, some "chiefs" at forts along the Missouri agreed to opening the Bozeman Trail. These chiefs were recognized by the U.S. government but not by their own people.

During this period, Red Cloud spoke most often for the Lakotas, primarily the Oglalas. Red Cloud made it clear that any whites passing the Dry Fork of the Powder would have to fight.

Colonel H. B. Carrington of the U.S. Army then received orders to begin building posts along the trail. Carrington undertook his mission with only seven hundred infantry, including musicians, but no cavalry. The year before, General P. E. Connor had carried on a war in the Powder River Country with three thousand cavalry. All the tribes he met remained there, except the southern Cheyennes, who had been removed from the area as a result of the war. Yet Carrington's actions and statements indicate he expected no major problem in taking the most important hunting grounds of the Arapahoes, Cheyennes, and Lakotas. Forty miles (65 kilometers) from Fort Reno, Carrington began construction of Fort Philip Kearny.

By the time summer ceremonies were concluded, meat for the winter had been gathered, and the snow fell, a thousand lodges of Lakotas, northern Cheyennes, and a few Blue Clouds camped together in the foothills near Fort Kearny. In December, they were ready to start new attacks on the fort.

Warrior leaders Crazy Horse and Hump began to devise new approaches to conducting warfare. The people could no longer afford the losses caused by traditional ways of battle, such as each warrior making his own decision when to attack, showing bravery by walking alone into the line of fire, or counting coup by striking an enemy without killing him. Instead, Crazy Horse and Hump devised a strategy whereby only a few warriors would show themselves. The rest would wait, hidden, until a leader determined it was time for all to move together, such as when the government soldiers were in a vulnerable position. Hump and Crazy Horse harangued their men for a long time about using patience, a decoy, and the tactic of surprise in the attack. One U.S. officer, Captain William Fetterman, had bragged publicly that he could ride through the Lakota nation with eighty men. This also fired up the warriors. Red Cloud called on a Miniconjou dreamer (spiritual adviser) to tell how the battle would turn out. The dreamer returned from his prayers to report he held one hundred dead white soldiers in his hand.

Early on the morning of December 21, 1866, the warriors followed Peno Creek to the end of Lodge Trail Ridge. They watched a wagon train come out of the fort with armed escorts led by Captain Fetterman. The decoys headed toward the wagon train. The other warriors waited, wondering if their new approach would work. They could not know that Carrington also waited with misgivings. He gave Fetterman his orders sternly and explicitly: "Support the wood train. Relieve it and report to me. Do not engage or pursue over Lodge Trail Ridge." He repeated the orders and then gave them to Fetterman in writing. Instead of advancing directly to the "wood train" (wagon train), however, Fetterman and his forces headed straight for Lodge Trail Ridge.

The hidden warriors waited as the soldiers followed their decoys. Crazy Horse took great risks, luring them closer and closer to the waiting warriors. The Lakotas and Cheyennes remained hidden and silent until Cheyenne Chief Little Horse gave the signal. Once Fetterman ordered his men to pursue the decoys, it was too late for him to figure out how to get any of his eighty-two men to safety. Many died before they ever fired a shot. Almost all turned to flee, with the cavalry leaving the foot soldiers behind. Still, they stayed bunched together, making it easy for the warriors to hit them with arrows.

A photographic portrait of Red Cloud, the Lakota leader who fought the encroachment by settlers, immigrants, and miners eager to get rich off of gold found on tribal land.

Ten Lakotas, two Cheyennes, and a Blue Cloud lay dead and more were injured, but the Miniconjous' dream proved true. Lakotas still call the Battle at Fort Philip Kearny the Battle of a Hundred Slain or the Battle of the Hundred in the Hand. Descendants of a man who got his name from the battle, Kills a Hundred, now live on the Pine Ridge Reservation. A monument the U. S. government erected at the battle site tells about the defeat of the three commissioned officers and seventy-six privates of the 18th U. S. Infantry and the 2nd U.S. Cavalry, along with four civilians. The end of the inscription reads, "There were no survivors."

During another fight in August of that year, the soldiers defended themselves successfully with their new breech-loading rifles. Despite the defeat of the

Lakota, government officials in Washington, D.C., understood that Red Cloud had no plans to end his war to protect the Powder River Country. Any soldier who ventured even a few paces from the camps would likely be killed, and the Lakotas burned most of the wagon trains and ran off with the horses. In less than a year, 150 white people had been killed. Although the army and its generals wanted to launch an all-out war against the Cheyennes and

Lakotas, government leaders decided a long, drawn-out war would be too costly and too unpopular. The situation seemed at a stalemate. The government kept asking for a peace treaty, non-Indians kept invading Lakota lands, and Red Cloud kept refusing "to touch the pen" (sign the treaty) until all the forts and the Bozeman Trail closed down. Finally, the forts closed down.

The Lakotas had won most of the battles and dictated the terms of peace, but in the end, they lost the war. Railroad tracks eventually crossed the Plains, and the soldiers and miners broke a new road starting farther west of Fort Laramie. Now the invaders did not really need the Bozeman Trail.

— C. Hamilton

Beth Brant, a Bay of Quinte Mohawk, is an accomplished poet and storyteller. In 1989, she edited an important anthology of writing and art by Native women titled *A Gathering of Spirit*.

SEE ALSO:
Coup Sticks, or Counting Coup; Crazy Horse; Epidemic Diseases; Red Cloud; Smallpox.

BRANT, BETH (1941–)

Beth Brant is a Bay of Quinte Mohawk from Tyendinaga Mohawk Territory in Ontario, Canada, who divides her time between living in Michigan and Canada. She is a widely published poet, storyteller, lecturer, and editor. Brant acted as editor of a groundbreaking collection of writing and art by Native women, *A Gathering of Spirit* (1989). She was also a guest coeditor in 1994 of a Native American literature special edition of *Callaloo*, a literary quarterly sponsored by the University of Virginia and published by Johns Hopkins University Press. She also serves on the National Advisory Caucus for Wordcraft Circle of Native Writers and Storytellers and delivered a plenary session speech at Returning the Gift, an historic gathering of nearly four hundred Native literary writers from throughout the upper Western Hemisphere, at the University of Oklahoma in 1992.

Her work has been included in many anthologies, including, most recently, *Returning the Gift: Poetry and Prose from the First North American Native Writers' Festival* (1994); *The Colour of Resistance: A Contemporary Collection of Writing by Aboriginal Women* (1993); *Kitchen Talk: An Anthology of Canadian Women's Prose and Poetry* (1992); *Getting Wet* (1992); *An Anthology of Native Canadian Literature in English* (1992); *Talking Leaves: Contemporary Native American Short Stories* (1991); and *Piece of My Heart* (1991).

Her own books include *Mohawk Trail* (1985) and *Food & Spirits* (1991), both published by Firebrand Books. Brant is currently working on a book of essays about land and spirit. Her work has appeared in a wide variety of magazines and journals, and, in 1990, the Canadian Broadcasting Corporation adapted and aired one of her best-known short stories, "Turtle Gal."

Brant was a lecturer at the University of British Columbia in 1989 and 1990. In 1991, she gave presentations at the Michigan Festival of Writers in East Lansing, Michigan, and at the Women of Color Writing Workshop in Vancouver, British Columbia. In 1992, she gave presentations at the Flight of the Mind Writing Workshop in Eugene, Oregon, and at the International Feminist Book Fair in Amsterdam, Holland. She has received grants from the Michigan Arts Council in 1984 and 1986 and from the Ontario Arts Council in 1989, and she received a fellowship from the National Endowment for the Arts in 1992. In 1993, she was writer in residence at the Kanhiote Library on the Tyendinaga Mohawk Reserve and was guest lecturer in women's studies and Native studies at New College, University of Toronto.

SEE ALSO:
Returning the Gift.

BRANT, JOSEPH (1742–1807)

Joseph Brant (Mohawk), also known as Thayendanegea, was prominent on the New York frontier during the mid-1700s as an Iroquois leader and an ally of the British in the American Revolution. His grandfather, Sa Ga Yean Qua Prah Ton, was one of the four "American kings" who were invited to London to visit Queen Anne's court in 1710.

In 1755, at the age of thirteen, Brant was present with William Johnson, British Indian agent, and other Mohawk allies at the Battle of Lake George. When the war with the French ended in 1763, Brant, who was still a young man, was tutored by Eleazer Wheelock at the Indian Charity School in Lebanon, Connecticut. The school would later be moved to New Hampshire and become known as Dartmouth College. He was an able student but dropped out after a year. Brant was married for a time to Margaret, a daughter of the Oneida sachem Skenandoah. After Margaret's death, Brant married Catherine Croghan, the Mohawk daughter of

George Croghan, the British Indian agent who was a close friend of William Johnson.

By 1765, Brant had settled in the Mohawk Valley and was translating the Gospel According to St. Mark into Mohawk. He also accepted a job as a secretary to Johnson and acquired farmland, cattle, and an interest in a gristmill. As personal secretary to Johnson, Brant became known as the most able interpreter available to the British in northeastern North America. As a Mohawk leader, Brant attended meetings of the Iroquois Grand Council at Onondaga and provided firsthand intelligence to the British military.

After William Johnson died in 1774, Brant became secretary to his nephew Guy Johnson, who had taken over the Indian superintendency for the Crown of England. In November, 1775, Brant sailed for England with Johnson. Brant made a favorable impression upon society in London. "As a Pine Tree Chief of the Iroquois, he wore knee-high moccasins and a blanket draped over one shoulder," wrote Frank Waters, author of *Brave Are My People*. "And as Col. Guy Johnson's secretary, he was equally at home in starched linen and broadcloth."

As further evidence of his popularity in England, a story about Brant appeared in the July 1776 edition of *London Magazine*, just as American revolutionaries were posting their Declaration of Independence in Philadelphia. (Londoners did not know this had happened until mid-August). On another visit to London in 1785, Brant was sought after by the celebrated author James Boswell, and he sat for a portrait by noted artist George Romney. Brant also dined with the Prince of Wales. He fascinated the English since he spoke their language well and had a European education. He was also a staunch churchman, a Mason, and a translator of the Bible into his native tongue. The British government treated him like a visiting statesman, providing him with personal guides to the sights of London.

During the Revolutionary War, Brant played a major role in rallying some of the Iroquois to the British cause. Brant had been told that some Mohawk lands would be returned to them if they allied with the British. Returning to America, he recruited most of the Mohawks, Senecas, Cayugas, and Onondagas to support the British; most of the Oneidas and Tuscaroras supported the revolution-

Joseph Brant, a Mohawk, was a prominent Iroquois leader in the middle of the eighteenth century. During the conflict between England and its enemies in North America, he became an ally of the British. On his visits to England, he impressed the citizens of London with his command of English and his European education.

warded by both sides. The British discarded their Mohawk, Onondaga, Cayuga, and Seneca allies at the earliest convenience. The Americans did the same to their own allies, the Tuscaroras and Oneidas. At the conclusion of the Revolutionary War, the border between the new United States and Canada (still under British dominion) was drawn straight through the middle of Iroquois country, without consulting the Indians.

Brant emigrated to British Canada with a number of Mohawks and other Iroquois, along with many Tories, who were non-Indian British sympathizers. The British military maintained Brant's rank at half pay and granted him land along the Grand River in Ontario, the site, today, of the Grand River Iroquois Council. Brant visited England again in 1786, at the Court of St. James. He devoted many of his later years to translating the Bible and other religious works into Mohawk and to raising seven children by three wives. He died November 24, 1807.

— B. E. Johansen

SEE ALSO:

American Revolution; Hendrick; Iroquois Confederacy; Johnson, Sir William; Mohawk.

aries. For the first time in several hundred years, the Iroquois League was split.

Brant's ferocity as a warrior was legendary; many settlers who supported the Americans called him "Monster Brant." The revolutionaries were no less fierce; revolutionary forces often adopted a scorched-earth policy against Iroquois who supported the British. That is, they attempted to burn Iroquois villages down to the ground. The battle for the Mohawk Valley ended when George Washington's forces defeated the British and their Iroquois allies at the battle of Johnstown.

Although the war had ended along the American frontier, the efforts of the Iroquois went unre-

BRENDALE V. CONFEDERATED TRIBES AND BAND OF YAKIMA

In 1989, the Supreme Court of the United States decided whether an Indian nation or the county—a subdivision within the state—has the authority to decide how a piece of reservation land is to be used by people owning it. This authority to "zone," as it is called, allows communities to control where property owners can build houses, farms, stores, and other businesses. As U.S. Supreme Court Justice John Paul Stevens noted, zoning "is the process whereby a community defines its essential character." In other words, zoning laws allow communities to keep farms from appearing in downtown areas or too many businesses from sprouting up in quiet neighborhoods.

In this case, Philip Brendale (a Yakima Indian by descent) and Stanley Wilkinson (a non-Indian) each wanted to divide his property on the reservation into smaller lots to sell them as cabin sites and homes. Brendale's land was in a part of the reservation known as "closed," because it was closed to all except members of the Yakima Nation and those whom the tribe allowed on the land. Wilkinson's land was on the "open" area of the reservation, which was owned and used by Indians and non-Indians alike. The Yakima Nation had zoned both of these properties to prevent the owners from building homes, but the county had zoned these areas so that both owners could build homes.

The Yakima Nation argued that an 1855 treaty with the U.S. government had granted it the power to zone all lands within the borders of its reservation. According to this treaty, the lands "will be set apart . . . for the exclusive use and benefit" of the Yakima. The treaty also states that no "white man, excepting those in the employment of the Indian Department, [shall] be permitted to reside upon the said reservation without permission of the tribe." In the case of Wilkinson (the non-Indian), the Supreme Court disagreed, arguing that the treaty is no longer valid because of the effects of the Allotment Act of 1887.

The Allotment Act allowed government officials to divide Indian lands into plots—usually of 160 acres (65 hectares)—and to distribute these plots to members of the tribe. In this way, Congress hoped to eliminate the Indian nations by making Indian people individual landowners like non-Indians, instead of letting them be part of an Indian nation with a large land base. After a number of years, some tribal members who received allotments sold their land to non-Indian people, creating areas (usually around towns) where many non-Indian people lived and owned property.

The Supreme Court held that in such areas where large numbers of non-Indian people live, the tribe cannot zone their property. On the other hand, in the case of Brendale (the Yakima property owner), the court held that the Yakima Nation does have the right to zone his property because the land is in the closed part of the reservation where few non-Indian people live.

The decision is controversial for a number of reasons. For one thing, the court affirmed the Allotment Act of 1887, which was intended to eliminate Native tribes. Yet the court's reasoning goes against the Congressional Indian Reorganization Act of 1934, which affirms the right of Native people to self-government, thereby overturning the letter and spirit of the antitribal Allotment Act. The court's decision also goes against a long-standing tradition of the Supreme Court allowing Native nations to have the jurisdiction, or authority, to rule on such civil matters as zoning on reservations where both Indian and non-Indian people live.

Finally, the decision makes it very difficult for lower courts to decide when enough non-Indian people reside on an area of a reservation to place it into the category of Wilkinson and not Brendale.

SEE ALSO:
General Allotment Act; Indian New Deal (Indian Reorganization Act of 1934); Tribal Sovereignty.

BRESETTE, WALTER (c. 1948–)

Walter Bresette is a Lake Superior Chippewa and noted lecturer who makes his home on the Red Cliff Reservation in Wisconsin. He is the coauthor, along with Rick Whaley, of a book entitled *Walleye Warriors: An Effective Alliance Against Racism and for the Earth* (with a foreword by Winona LaDuke). This book, published in 1994, provides a Native American viewpoint on the controversy over spearfishing, a traditional method of fishing. Spearfishing is protected by treaties with the United States, but it has been met with strenuous protests by non-Natives in the upper Midwest.

In 1983, in the *Voigt* decision, the Indian spearfishers won the right in court to practice their traditional methods of fishing, but that proved to be only the beginning of their problems. Imagine trying to launch your boat to go fishing while the police at the landing hold back howling mobs that throw rocks and shout insults, racial slurs, and death threats. Add to that the knowledge that the police and other state authorities consider not the howling mob, but you, the spearfisher, to be the problem, and you begin to see what happens even when Indians win in court. As Walter Bresette says, "They [the non-Natives] reacted as if manifest destiny had been overturned."

In *Walleye Warriors*, Bresette describes the controversy over spearfishing, emphasizing the Native American point of view. But the book is more than just a chronicle of the violent backlash against spearfishers following the 1983 *Voigt* decision. It is also a blueprint for how Native peoples in other parts of the continent can meet the threats of intimidation when they have successfully asserted their rights in court.

This method concerns the highly successful Witness for Non-Violence program, in which people are schooled in the art of observing and recording racial hatred. People committing racist acts, especially acts of violence, do not like to have their acts witnessed or recorded by others not involved in the conflict. They know that such acts are against the law. Being a boat-landing Witness was a risky business. However, many people have become trained in this art, some from as far away as Germany.

In addition to giving a detailed account of events concerning spearfishing in Wisconsin from 1983 to 1992, *Walleye Warriors* also traces the history of the modern anti-Indian treaty movement to its roots in the 1960s and 1970s in the state of Washington. It also has much to say about such interwoven issues as Indian treaty rights and the mining threat. The book has many other things to offer as well, ranging from a brief history of the Anishinabe (Ojibwe) to observations and impressions of organizers of the American Indian Movement in northern Wisconsin in the 1970s.

Rick Whaley and Walter Bresette helped co-found a number of groups, including Witness for Non-Violence, the Midwest Treaty Network, and Anishinabe Niijii—a mining watchdog group. Whaley is editor of the *Witness Training Manual*.

SEE ALSO:
Fishing Rights; Manifest Destiny.

BRITISH COLUMBIA

In 1986, British Columbia's on-reserve population of First Nations People was 30,045. Total off-reserve populations were 96,260, most of whom resided in the numerous urban centers throughout this Canadian province.

Along the north coast are found the Gitskan, Nishga, Haida, Tsimshian, and Haisla. Along the west-central coast are found the Bella Coola, Heiltsuk, Kwawgewlth (Kwakiutl), and Nuu-chah-nulth (Nootka or West Coast). Along the south coast are found the Comox, Island Cowichan, Songish, Fraser, Halkomelem, Sechelt, Squamish, Semiahmoo, and Puntlatch. In the northern interior of British Columbia are found the Inland Tlingit, Kaska, Tahltan, Beaver, Sekani, and Slave; in the central interior are found the Carrier, Chilcotin, Shuswap, and Lillooet. And in the southern interior are found the Thompson, Okanagan, and Kootenay.

Linguistically, the two largest groups inhabiting the province are the Athabaskan (or Dene') and the Salish. These two peoples are divided roughly by a line running southwest from the Alberta-British Columbia border in the headwaters of the Fraser River to a point between the heads of Bute and Knight Inlet.

The Dene' are subdivided into several groups within the province: the Tahltan, Kaska, and Slave in the north; the Beaver and Sekani in the central portion of the area; and, farther south, the Carrier (or Takulli) and Chilcotin.

The Salish group, in the southern area of British Columbia, are subdivided into two major divisions, Coast Salish and Interior Salish. The Interior Salish have been subdivided into the Shuswap of the eastern interior, the Lillooet of the Anderson Lake and Lillooet River areas, and the Thompson and Okanagan of the district just north of the U.S. border between the Columbia and Fraser Rivers.

A third linguistic group are the Kootenay, who inhabit the extreme southeastern corner of the province. Originally migrants from the central plains, the Kootenay use a language that carries elements of both Algonquian and Sioux tongues.

On the western half of Vancouver Island, the Nootka culture stretches from the Port Renfrew area in the south to Quatsino Sound in the north. These people, speaking a variety of dialects, belong to a linguistic division known as the Wakashan, to which also belong the Kwakiutl people of northeastern Vancouver Island and the adjacent mainland coastal area. The habitat of the Kwakiutl people is divided in two by an isolated group of the Salish known as the Bella Coola.

The Tsimshian inhabit the mainland and coastal archipelago near the Nass and Skeena Rivers. The Haida inhabit the Queen Charlotte Islands and the southern portion of Prince of Wales Island.

SEE ALSO:
Alberta.

BRITISH COLUMBIA ASSOCIATION OF NON-STATUS INDIANS

In 1969, H. A. "Butch" Smitheram, a nonstatus Indian from Penticton, British Columbia (B.C.), Canada, founded the British Columbia Association of Non-Status Indians (BCANSI). Membership and voting privileges were open to any nonstatus person (that is, a person not a member of a tribe recognized by the Canadian government) of one-quarter or more Indian blood. Activities were organized around local community chapters, or "locals," and soon BCANSI had over seventy active locals.

Originally, the intent of BCANSI was to bring about changes in Canadian laws so that nonstatus Indians and Métis (mixed-blood) people would be entitled to the same benefits and services as status Indians who lived on the reserves. The British Columbia First Citizens' Fund provided much of the original funding for the organization. Fred House, a Métis from Alberta, soon replaced Butch Smitheram as president of the organization.

As the early 1970s unfolded, however, activism by Native people in B.C. began to increase. Many who were not happy with, nor eligible for, status services on-reserve put increasing pressure on the Native organizations in B.C., including BCANSI. In the 1972 annual BCANSI assembly, Bill Wilson, a status Native employee of BCANSI, proposed in a document that all persons of Indian

With a long Pacific coastline, many of British Columbia's Native people are also maritime people. This Indian village at Port Simpson, British Columbia, is located on the Inside Passage.

This ornately carved totem stands in Stanley Park, in Vancouver, British Columbia.

ancestry were entitled to share in lands claims. This was similar to the goal of the Union of B.C. Indian Chiefs, which represented the status Indians.

In 1975, BCANSI voted to reject government funding (as did the Union of B.C. Indian Chiefs) and to merge with the union. Bill Lightbown was the BCANSI president during this time. The Union of B.C. Indian Chiefs then closed its offices and laid off its staff, which made it possible for activist workers to pursue their goals in other ways throughout the province. Thus, the rejection of government funding permanently altered the political landscape of Native politics in British Columbia. By 1976, when BCANSI returned to government funding, its membership had been opened to status Indians. This change in direction and orientation led to the renaming of BCANSI in 1977 as the United Native Nations (UNN), with Bill Wilson as the new president.

George Watts, a political ally and personal friend of Bill Wilson, became active within the UNN. Soon, changing alliances created hostilities between the Union of B.C. Indian Chiefs and the UNN. The union felt threatened by both the activism and the different organizational structure of the UNN. The UNN was organized so that individual members could have direct input into the decisions of the organization. The union, on the other hand, had a more centralized leadership, with decisions being made by elected band chiefs within the union. Within the UNN, leadership and community involvement were the two qualities asked of anyone who wanted to participate, either at the local or the provincial levels. Since membership was voluntary, the members tended to be open to new ideas, ideas to which they were willing to commit both time and energy.

In 1976, a federal cabinet directive instructed the Department of Indian Affairs and Northern Development (DIAND) to consult all major groups representing status Indians. Fred Walchli, the Director of DIAND's B.C. Region, assisted in the development of a regional forum. In 1980, the UNN was asked to become an active participant in the forum. Subsequently, the forum asked DIAND and the secretary of state to stop recognizing the Union of B.C. Indian Chiefs as the sole recipient of funds intended for status Indians. The forum asked that such funds be granted instead on the basis of pro-

portional popular support to district/tribal councils and provincial organizations.

In 1980, Bob Warren succeeded the retiring Bill Wilson as president of the UNN. In the same year, the UNN became a full member of the Native Council of Canada. In 1982, the UNN participated in a Native Council meeting and voted to accept the Nishga policy statement on aboriginal rights as applicable to the whole province.

In the 1980s, the UNN devoted a great deal of energy, time, and money to building local chapters, developing leadership among youth, and regaining status-Indian membership by Indian women, who had lost their status because of DIAND's enforcement of regulations under the Indian Act.

UNN leadership changed hands several times. Among the leaders were Ron George and Dan Smith, who was president in 1995, both of whom are nationally recognized and involved in the leadership of Native communities.

As of the early 1990s, the UNN had grouped its locals into nine provincial zones. Each local is independent, with the UNN Head Office in Vancouver supplying support and guidance upon request. The UNN Head Office is active in housing, employment and training, and fee-for-service government contracts, among other activities.

— G. William

SEE ALSO:
Bill C-31; British Columbia; Métis.

BROWN, DEE ALEXANDER (1908–)

Dee Brown was born in Louisiana on February 28, 1908, but spent his boyhood in Arkansas. A non-Native author, during his career as a librarian he began researching and writing historical books. Brown has a deep personal interest in nineteenth-century western history and in American Indians, both of which became the focus of some twenty-six books and many articles. Brown's nonfiction works are noted for their excellent research.

Brown's most ambitious and successful historical work is *Bury My Heart at Wounded Knee*, a chronicle of the colonizing of the West from the viewpoint of Native Americans, who were victims of the Manifest Destiny doctrine in effect during the book's

1860–1890 time span. Brown used primary-source material such as treaty council records, recorded speeches, and autobiographies of Indians who lived during the time. Published in 1971, the book became a best-seller, with over one million copies sold.

Publication of *Bury My Heart at Wounded Knee* coincided with a general interest in ethnic studies in the United States in the early 1970s. Furthermore, its account of the harsh treatment suffered by Native people at the hands of U.S. troops and settlers struck a chord in the American psyche after the massacre of villagers in My Lai by U.S. troops during the war in Vietnam. Although labeled as "revisionist history" for being written from a viewpoint different from widely accepted historical works, the careful documentation of each event makes it impossible to deny the book's message.

Brown also wrote several historical novels. *Creek Mary's Blood* (1980) is a multigenerational epic that uses one family's story to illustrate several historical events, including the Trail of Tears, Little Bighorn, and Wounded Knee. The novel has been criticized for having stilted dialogue and for promoting historical inaccuracies regarding Creek Mary, an actual person. Brown's attempt to present the Indian perspective in this story misses the mark, according to several Native American critics.

SEE ALSO:
Little Bighorn, Battle of the; Manifest Destiny; Trail of Tears; Wounded Knee (1890).

BROWNE, VEE (1956–)

Vee Browne (Navajo) is an award-winning author of children's books who lives in the Navajo Nation near Chinle in northeastern Arizona. Browne gained national recognition when her first children's book, *Monster Slayer*, a retelling of a traditional Navajo story, won the 1991 Western Heritage Award from the Cowboy Hall of Fame and Western Heritage Center in Oklahoma City, Oklahoma. She soon produced a sequel, *Monster Birds*. Both books were published by Northland Publishing Company of Flagstaff, Arizona.

Browne has been a guidance counselor and teacher in the Navajo Nation school system, a writer

for the *Navajo-Hopi Observer*, and a lecturer who has also participated in television productions regarding Native American topics. Her work has appeared in such publications as *Moccasin Telegraph* and the internationally distributed *ELF: Eclectic Literary Forum*. Her essays have been anthologized in *Neon Powwow: New Native American Voices of the Southwest*, which was edited by Anna Lee Walters, a well-known Native American writer who teaches at Navajo Community College. Browne's latest book, *Maria Tallchief*, is a children's biography of the famous Osage ballerina, which was published in 1995 by Modern Curriculum Press, an educational publishing division of Simon and Schuster.

Browne is also active in helping beginning and emerging Native American writers learn their craft and find outlets for their work, serving on the National Advisory Caucus for Wordcraft Circle of Native American Writers and Storytellers. In 1995, she teamed with noted Navajo poet Laura Tohe, who also serves on the Wordcraft Circle National Advisory Caucus, in sponsoring a workshop for Native writers set in the spectacular natural beauty of Canyon de Chelly National Monument near Chinle. Recently, Browne has turned her attention to writing scripts for documentaries, working on her first novel, and pursuing postgraduate study at the University of Arizona.

BRUCHAC, JOSEPH (1942–)

Joseph Bruchac, an enrolled member of the Abenaki Nation of Vermont, St. Francis Sokoki Band, is also of Slovak and English heritage. Born in 1942, he founded the Greenfield Review Press in New York state, where he has been a leading publisher of American Indian and multiethnic literature. His own work has been published in more than five hundred publications, including more than fifty books for adults and children, and in collections of writings by American Indian authors.

From 1960 to 1965, he attended Cornell University, where he was also a heavyweight varsity wrestler. He earned a bachelor's degree in English with a minor in wildlife conservation. In 1966, he earned a master's degree at Syracuse University and then spent the next three years teaching in Ghana,

Joseph Bruchac, a member of the Abenaki Nation of Vermont, is a prolific American Indian poet, editor, novelist, publisher, and storyteller. In 1992, he chaired the first gathering of North American Indian creative writers, a weeklong conference at the University of Oklahoma called Returning the Gift.

West Africa. In 1974, after years of study, he earned his Ph.D. in comparative literature from the Union Institute in Ohio. During the next decade, he taught at several universities, including Skidmore College, Hamilton College, Columbia University, and the State University of New York at Albany.

In 1992, Bruchac helped organize the first-ever North American Native writers' festival, called Returning the Gift, held in Norman, Oklahoma, where nearly four hundred people attended. In his lifetime, he has received many awards for his writing and leadership. They include the Benjamin Franklin Award as "Person of the Year" in 1993 from the Publisher's Marketing Association and the Hope S. Dean Award for Notable Achievement in Children's Literature.

Bruchac currently lives in Greenfield Center, New York, in the Adirondack Mountain foothills with his wife, Carol, and two sons, James and Jesse, where he continues to write. He is also a member of the DawnLand Singers, a group of Abenaki singers and musicians, most of them Bruchac family members, whose aim, as stated in the notes to one of their albums, *Alnobak,* "is to entertain and educate, to represent a small part of the strength of . . . living Native people" of the Abenaki Nation.

SEE ALSO:
Returning the Gift.

BUFFALO

The buffalo was the most important resource of the Great Plains tribes; they depended on it for their very survival. The buffalo, or bison, belongs to the same family as the cow, the bovine family. Although estimates vary, pioneer naturalists estimated that buffalo numbered about sixty million at the time of the first European contact with North America. The greatest concentration of buffalo was on the plains and prairies, from the Rocky Mountains to the Mississippi River and from the Great Slave Lake in Canada to Texas. The buffalo dominated the land. During the early 1800s, one vast herd was estimated to be twenty-five miles (forty kilometers) across and fifty miles (eighty kilometers) long. It took the herd five days to cross a given point of land.

An adult male stands 7 feet tall (2.1 meters) at the shoulders and is nearly 12 feet (3.6 meters) long, weighing up to a ton (0.9 metric ton). The buffalo have long, thick, curly, brownish black hair on their heads, necks, and shoulders and a short, tufted tail. The hair on the hindquarters is shorter and grayish brown. The hair on the face of the bull can sometimes be 4–5 inches (11–13 centimeters) thick, and hair forms a beard at the throat and chin as well. The buffalo's hump is made of solid muscle to support its heavy head; the horns are sharp and curving.

The buffalo provided everything needed to maintain a comfortable, healthy life. The buffalo is held sacred by Plains people. All the Plains tribes held important religious ceremonies to honor the source of all their blessings. The buffalo made it easy to live on the Plains. Wherever the herd traveled, the hunters followed.

The hunt was a very important part of Plains life. Often a young boy would come into manhood by killing his first buffalo. In earlier times, the Plains people developed various hunting techniques while hunting on foot. These included using a bow, arrow, and lance. Hunting parties on foot herded the buffalo toward a cliff or started a prairie fire to stampede the herd over the cliff so the buffalo would be killed or crippled. These sites are called "buffalo jumps."

With the arrival of the horse and firearms, the Plains tribes' hunting practices and lifestyles were revolutionized. A hunter on a trained horse could easily run down a running buffalo. The hunters developed a highly successful method of hunting the buffalo. While on horseback, they formed two semicircles on each side of the herd, thus confusing the buffalo. This method was called "horse surround."

The buffalo were hunted all year around, but the great hunts occurred in September, when the warm summer weather was turning cool, and in April, when winter was ending. In these seasons, the cows were fat and would provide lots of good meat, and all buffalo had thick hides that would make warm robes.

Before a hunt, scouts were sent out to find the herds and estimate their numbers. Then hunters rode to the site on specially trained horses. These horses were guided by the rider's knees so his hands and arms would be free to aim and shoot on target. After a hunt, the rest of the people arrived at the site, bringing knives for skinning and butchering.

A bison cow and calf in Alberta, Canada. Bison, or buffalo, as they are popularly called, once ranged across the plains of North America in vast herds. They were hunted nearly to extinction by white buffalo hunters, partly for the value of their hides, and partly as a policy of the U.S. Army to destroy the food supply of the Plains Indians.

Buffalo Bill Cody began his career as a Pony Express rider, became a buffalo hunter for the railroads, and ended his career as a showman. Less well known today are his activities as a scout for the U.S. Army. In 1872, he received the Congressional Medal of Honor for his participation in aggression against Native people.

were made from the hump. Toys, tools, and needles were made from the bones. The muscles along the buffalo's backbone, called sinew, were used as thread. Spoons and cups were made from the horns. The stomach and bladder of the buffalo could make a good pot and also could carry food and water. Dried buffalo droppings were used as fuel for campfires. Buffalo hair was used for making ropes, belts, and decorations. Buffalo fat was used as soap, hair dressing, and pemmican, a food made from dried meat, fat, and berries.

As more and more settlers moved west, between 1872 and 1878, the buffalo population sharply declined and almost became extinct. Getting rid of the buffalo was a tactic used by the U.S. government to subdue the Plains Indians. The U.S. Army supplied commercial hunters with ammunition and offered to buy buffalo hides for $3.50 each. A buffalo "hunter" would shoot and skin forty to sixty buffalo a day.

Today, fewer than one hundred thousand buffalo remain in North America. They live on private ranches and in parks, zoos, and preserves in the United States and Canada.

— T. Midge

It was important that every part of the buffalo should be used—nothing should be wasted. A buffalo not only provided meat, it also provided the materials for hundreds of different uses. Shields

BUFFALO BILL CODY (1846–1917)

Buffalo Bill Cody is best known as a legendary figure in American showmanship. He was a notorious buffalo hunter on the western frontier as well as a scout and guide for the U.S. military, a Pony Express rider, a hunter, an author, and a showman.

William Frederick Cody, his given name, was born in 1846 in Scott County, Iowa. At the age of fourteen, he became one of the youngest riders for the Pony Express. At eighteen, he joined the Union Army during the Civil War; he later became a scout for General William Tecumseh Sherman, commander of the Union troops, and fought against Indians. Credited with having killed four thousand buffalo, Cody earned his famous nickname, "Buffalo Bill," by providing buffalo meat for railroad workers. He once astonished five army officers by killing eleven buffalo with just twelve shots.

Cody's name became famous across the country, and in 1872 he was awarded the Congressional Medal of Honor for his ruthless participation in wars of aggression against Native people. His fame led to a lucrative stage career that was interrupted by more fighting over the invasion of the Black Hills by gold miners, which broke the provisions of the 1868 Treaty of Fort Laramie between the U.S. government and the Sioux.

Later, Cody created Buffalo Bill's Wild West Show. This spectacular theatrical program employed cowboys, trick shooters, and famous Indian warriors such as Sitting Bull. The show toured through every major city in the United States and also Europe, making Buffalo Bill a millionaire. He died on January 10, 1917, at the age of seventy-one. To many who witnessed or learned of Cody's slaughter of buffalo and his exhibitions exploiting Native people and cultures, his life symbolizes the extent to which racism against Native people and their cultures could be used to provide fame and fortune to showmen like Cody.

SEE ALSO:
Buffalo Bill's Wild West Show.

BUFFALO BILL'S WILD WEST SHOW

From 1883 through the first part of the twentieth century, William Frederick Cody, also known as Buffalo Bill, made grand, sweeping tours throughout the United States and Europe with his Wild West Show extravaganza. His spectacular shows fascinated audiences, young and old, by reenacting famous cavalry and Plains Indian wars and romanticizing other events in American history.

His shows were also blatantly exploitative of Native peoples and cultures, playing on familiar stereotypes and creating some new ones concerning the relationship between Indians, whites, and various other groups out on the Plains. One of his Wild West Show posters, for example, depicts an unruly gang of horsemen described as a "Congress of Rough Riders of the World." Some can be identified as cowboys and Indians; others fit the popular images of the day of Arabs, South American cowboys, called *gauchos*, and European cavalrymen. In the forefront is Buffalo Bill, the master of what is further described on the poster as an exhibition dramatizing the "Rivalries of Savage, Barbarous and Civilized Races."

The Wild West Show was inaugurated in Omaha in 1883 with "real" cowboys and Indians portraying what most Americans like to think of as the "real West." The show spent ten of its thirty years in Europe. In 1887, Buffalo Bill was a featured attraction at Queen Victoria's Golden Jubilee in England. The phenomenal success of the Wild West Show was founded on a nostalgia for the passing of the "frontier," a nostalgia that swept the nation in the late nineteenth century.

Buffalo Bill's Wild West Show was staged outdoors. The stage consisted of an arena large enough to contain buffalo, horses, bears, Texas longhorn steers, bucking broncos, Pony Express riders, stagecoach drivers, Conestoga wagons, Indian tepees, chiefs and warriors, and cowboys. The earliest show, called "Buffalo Bill's Wild West Rocky Mountain and Prairie Exhibition," was so large that it filled six boxcars, two open cars, and two coaches with all of its equipment.

At the center of it all stood Cody himself. He cut an imposing figure, wearing a white fringed and beaded buckskin suit and white sombrero, riding a white horse, and carrying a Winchester rifle. From its very first performance, in Omaha, Nebraska, on May 17, 1883, the show was a success.

One popular performer was the renowned sharpshooter Annie Oakley. She astounded audiences with her quick aim and impressive accuracy with a rifle. Oakley could slice a playing card in two and

For thirty years, Buffalo Bill's Wild West Show played to audiences in outdoor theaters in North America and in Europe. By 1918, it could no longer compete with movie theaters.

shoot an apple from her French poodle's head, cigarettes from her husband's mouth, and a dime held between his fingers.

Another featured performer was the famous Sioux leader, Sitting Bull. Playing himself, Sitting Bull participated in the reenactment of the Battle of the Little Bighorn. Sitting Bull and Cody got along well together; a photograph taken in Mon-

treal showed the two clasping hands with the caption reading, "Foes in '76, Friends in '85." Annie Oakley reportedly became a favorite of Sitting Bull as well. He is said to have nicknamed her "Little Sure Shot."

By 1918, the heyday of the successful Wild West exhibitions was drawing to a close, but certain acts continued to be featured in circuses, such as Barnum and Bailey's. By then, audiences were fascinated with a new medium—movies—and the western shows slowly faded out. In retrospect, it seems demeaning and cruelly ironic that Native people were made to have a part in the reenactment of their own conquest. Because their traditional way of life had been taken away from them, however, many Native Americans found themselves without a way of making a living. This was the greater cruelty that lay behind spectacles like Buffalo Bill's Wild West Show.

SEE ALSO:
Buffalo Bill Cody; Sitting Bull.

BUREAU OF AMERICAN ETHNOLOGY

The Bureau of American Ethnology (BAE) came into existence on March 3, 1879, when the U.S.

Congress combined several governmental agencies already in existence for the purpose of collecting and housing information about American Indians. In 1964, the BAE was merged with the Department of Anthropology, U.S. National Museum, to form the Smithsonian Office of Anthropology.

In 1879, the study of Native peoples was conducted in part through the United States Geological Survey, one of the BAE's component agencies. That the study of Native peoples was associated with geology demonstrates, in the view of many critics, that Indians were regarded as being a part of nature, rather than as human beings. That the BAE's first director, John Wesley Powell, was a major in the U.S. Army, suggests to many historians that the BAE's unstated purpose was to use the information gathered about Native peoples to U.S. military advantage in its wars against various Indian nations.

The BAE gathered a huge collection of information regarding Native peoples, published mainly in its *Annual Reports* and *Bulletins*. Eighty-one *Annual Reports* and 193 *Bulletins* were published between 1879 and 1964. The essays in these reports cover every area of anthropology, including ethnology, archaeology, and linguistics. Much of the information formed the foundation for later books about Native peoples.

The BAE's most prolific author, John R. Swanton, is a case in point for demonstrating that the BAE, to its credit, recorded a tremendous amount of information of historical value, yet was hampered by its own biases and racism in reporting the information. Over the course of his career, for example, Swanton wrote twenty short works (called monographs) while most of his contemporaries produced only one.

Many of Swanton's reports are monumental. For example, his work on the Creeks was published in the *Forty-second Annual Report*. It is a huge, encyclopedic work that records everything from linguistic details regarding the Creek language to the layout of the Creek square grounds. Yet Swanton's report is riddled with judgment and bias. In a section entitled "Native Explanations of Their Origin," Swanton states his belief that since many Native stories contain varying explanations for the same phenomenon, the stories must be unreliable

sources of information. For example, in a discussion of Native stories that explain how clans came into being and got their names, Swanton refers to the stories as "myths" and calls the differences in clan stories a "confusion."

Swanton's condescending attitude toward Native stories is amplified in later sections of the *Forty-second Annual Report*. He analyzes a Creek story of how the Bear and Wolf clans came into being in the following passage: "Of an entirely different type is the following trivial tale which pretends to account for the separation between the Bear and the Wolf [clans]." The words *trivial* and *pretends* show that Swanton had little respect for Native oral traditions.

Throughout the *Forty-second Annual Report*, Swanton felt it necessary to distinguish between what he considered the falsity of Indian accounts of their history and what he believed was the indisputable truth of the non-Native, European-centered version of history: "Any discussion of the probable origin and evolution of the Creek confederacy must carefully distinguish between the native conception regarding its origin and evolution and the thing itself; between the psychological construction and the actual facts."

In another passage, in a discussion of accounts of clans that are related to each other, he says, "As I shall have occasion to show more than once, Indians are most skillful in inventing reasons for institutions or customs already in existence. Native explanations of the association of the Bird and Beaver and the Bird and Alligator are examples. There are other linkings which might seem beyond Indian ingenuity to account for, yet I believe that reasons for such associations would be discovered by them."

Some scholars have pointed out that the use of words like *most skillful, inventing,* and *ingenuity* to describe Native explanations is condescending in its attitude toward Native oral traditions. They also point out that the use of these words ignores the fact that most of the world's religions have a variety of myths that explain the origins of and reasons behind phenomena in nature.

These samples of Swanton's attitudes are merely a few taken from a small number of pages in only one of Swanton's publications. They stand in contrast to the care that official documents must take today to give information in an accurate and culturally sensitive way. The fact that these statements were published in a U.S. government document shows that racist and condescending attitudes toward Indians were fully accepted by most non-Native Americans of Swanton's time.

Worse still, these negative attitudes were passed on to scholars who have used Swanton's work in their own research. For example, the *Forty-second Annual Report* was a major source of information for all the books written about Creeks for many decades after the report's publication. All of these books were influenced, some subtly, some more overtly, by Swanton's attitudes and biases.

Swanton's work is only one example. Many of the other researchers working and writing for the BAE had similar biases. For this reason, the BAE has had a far-reaching influence on authors of American Indian texts, and hence about what non-Native Americans and even Native peoples themselves believe about their cultures and their histories.

Some scholars have a less critical view of the BAE, pointing out that throughout its lifetime, the BAE employed many distinguished Native American intellectuals, such as George Bushotter, the Lakota ethnographer who wrote the first account of his people in their own language. These scholars also point out that many distinguished non-Native BAE authors, such as Frank Boas, were critics of racism and that their work helped pave the way for a more tolerant social atmosphere in the late twentieth century.

The passing of the BAE may be a cause for celebration, for mourning, or a little of both. In any case, the ethnographic works the BAE produced need to be read carefully and critically.

— C. S. Womack

SEE ALSO:
Bushotter, George; Creation Stories; Ethnography.

SUGGESTED READINGS:

Judd, Neil M. *The Bureau of American Ethnology: A Partial History*. Norman: University of Oklahoma Press, 1967.

Lurie, Nancy Oestreich. "Relations Between Indians and Anthropologists," *Handbook of North American Indians* (edited by William C. Sturtevant), vol. 4 (*History of Indian-White Relations*, edited by Wilcomb E. Washburn), pp. 548–56. Washington, D.C.: Smithsonian Institution, 1988.

Swann, Brian. *On the Translation of Native American Literatures*. Washington: Smithsonian Institution Press, 1992.

Swann, Brian. *Smoothing the Ground: Essays on Native American Oral Literature*. Berkeley: University of California Press, 1983.

BUREAU OF INDIAN AFFAIRS

When it was created in 1824, the Bureau of Indian Affairs (BIA) was a minor office in the U.S. War Department. In 1849, the BIA was transferred to the Department of the Interior, and it is still part of the Interior Department today.

Throughout its history, the Bureau of Indian Affairs has had shifts in its purpose and policies, reflecting the general changes in the U.S. government's policy toward American Indians. The extremes of these changes are most clearly seen in the policies of BIA head John Collier in the 1930s, who attempted to allow Native people to maintain some of their traditional cultural practices. Collier's leadership of the BIA sharply contrasts with BIA attempts in the 1950s to terminate the rights of Indians as sovereign nations. For most of its history, the BIA has followed a policy of encouraging or even forcing Indians to try to assimilate into American culture.

Although seen by much of society as an agency in which Native people may go for aid, the BIA historically has not been helpful to American Indians. Starting in the early 1800s, Native Americans were confined to reservations with government posts nearby, and the BIA was set up to be the watchdog over them. Indians had to rely on the BIA to provide for their needs, including food, clothing, and education.

For much of its history, the BIA has been plagued with corruption. During the 1800s, BIA food rations meant for people on the reservations were often illegally taken by other U.S. govern-

A group of about five hundred American Indians occupy an auditorium at the Bureau of Indian Affairs in Washington, D.C., on November 2, 1972. The occupation brought national attention to broken treaties and to desperate economic and health conditions on reservations.

ment agencies. Sometimes, the federal agencies gave the best meat and food to soldiers in the army. Other times, government officials sold the food to non-Indian settlers. Still other times, they kept the food for themselves. Indians, who had few other sources of food, sometimes tried to rob BIA food stores. If caught, they were jailed or, more often, executed for the crime of taking food that was actually meant for them.

Another way that the Bureau of Indian Affairs did a grave disservice to American Indians was through its educational policies. It was a BIA policy to try to force Indian children to give up their traditional ways and assimilate. To this end, the agency set up schools for young Natives far away from the reservations. Native children were required to leave their families and live at the BIA boarding schools. They were forbidden to speak their native languages and were severely disciplined for displaying any aspect of their traditional cultures.

In some instances, the children were placed in dungeonlike cells for disobeying these rules.

Hundreds of children at these schools suffered from severe loneliness. Many died from diseases or from injuries sustained due to the harsh discipline.

The BIA boarding schools have thus played a major role in Indian nations' losses of language and traditional ways. They have helped create a cultural division between traditional Indians and those who have accepted the culture of non-Native America.

Another way that the Bureau of Indian Affairs has helped to destroy Indian ways of life was with its policy promoting the establishment of Christian churches on reservations. In the 1860s, different Christian churches lobbied the BIA for the right to establish their churches on different reservations. One reservation might be assigned to the Roman Catholic Church, for example, while another might be assigned to the Methodist Church.

Most of these Christian churches forbade Native people from practicing their own religions. Indians therefore had to practice traditional religions in secret, hiding their dances and other religious ceremonies. The secrecy caused the general public to believe that the Indian religions were pagan or forms of devil worship. Even today, Native religions are not widely understood or appreciated by many non-Native Americans.

The Bureau of Indian Affairs is still the agency to "help" the Indians. In recent years, the BIA has promoted "self-governance" policies in which Indian nations are to maintain their governments and programs without aid from the U.S. government. This policy is in direct contradiction with Indian treaties.

In the face of self-governance, the BIA has not helped Native people fight against cases of double taxation or the illegal prosecution of Native religious acts. The agency has given Indians very little help in becoming self-sufficient. However, the BIA is still responsible for the education of Indian people. The agency administers programs in the public schools to help Indian students maintain their culture while obtaining a well-rounded education in reading, writing, and arithmetic.

— S. S. Davis

SEE ALSO:
Boarding Schools; Collier, John.

BUREAU OF LAND MANAGEMENT

In 1946, the U.S. government consolidated two agencies—the General Land Office (established in 1812) and the Grazing Service (established in 1934)—to form the Bureau of Land Management (BLM). The BLM's responsibility is to monitor and manage the use of land and resources on federal lands.

Indian reservations are considered federal lands. Thus, the policies of the BLM and its predecessors on such matters as water use, grazing, mining, and logging have greatly affected the lives of Native people. Because so many of the effects have been adverse ones, American Indians consider the BLM a major adversary in their struggle to gain their rights.

Many of the reservations created by the government were based around lakes or other large water sources. In time, the non-Indian population of the West grew, and the government was responsible for getting water to those people. In 1905, half of the Truckee River was diverted by the Derby Dam. The river had fed many lakes, including Pyramid Lake in the territory of the Paiute. With the building of Derby Dam, Pyramid Lake decreased in size by about 50 percent. Even though the Paiute had rights to the water, no one had asked or informed them about the effects of the dam on the water supply.

In addition to supplying western cities, water taken from Native people was, and is, used on farms and ranches that are owned by non-Indians. BLM policies with regard to grazing also have favored non-Indian farmers and ranchers over Indians. For example, in 1973, the Danns, a Western Shoshoni family of ranchers, were told that their cattle were trespassing on what the Bureau of Land Management considered public rangeland.

The BLM said the family had to purchase grazing permits. The family, under the leadership of Carrie and Mary Dann, refused to do so, pointing out that the Western Shoshoni had never agreed to cede their land to the government. As a result of their refusal to comply with the Bureau of Land Management, the Shoshoni ranchers had their cattle rounded up by federal agents and impounded.

The Bureau of Land Management oversees mining, logging, and other uses of natural resources. In this capacity, it has been responsible for the misuse and even the seizure of American Indian land. Many sacred sites have been devastated because valuable minerals have been found underground. The U.S. government claims that the minerals' importance to the country as a whole outweighs Indians' rights to maintain their sacred sites. In addition, mining on Indian land has caused an increase in illness among the people because of water contamination. The contamination also affects animals, leaving Native farmers and ranchers with less than healthy food.

SEE ALSO: Dann Sisters; Federal Lands; Sacred Sites.

BURIAL GROUNDS, INDIAN

SEE Reburial and Repatriation of Human Remains and Sacred Objects; Sacred Sites.

BUSH, BARNEY FURMAN (1944–)

Barney Bush (Shawnee-Cayuga) is a widely published poet and teacher. He was born in Saline Country, Illinois, in 1944. He studied graphic arts at the Institute of American Indian Art in Santa Fe , New Mexico, and he received a B.A. in humanities from Fort Lewis College in Durango, Colorado, and an M.A. in English and fine arts from the University of Idaho. He currently teaches creative writing at the Institute of American Indian Arts.

Bush shared the story of his life in "The Personal Statement of Barney Bush," in *I Tell You Now: Autobiographical Essays by Native American Writers* (1987). He has also published several collections of his poetry, including *Longhouse of the Blackberry Moon* (1975), *My Horse and a Jukebox*

(1979), *Petroglyphs* (1982), and *Inherit the Blood* (1985).

Bush's work has appeared in *Sun Tracks, Scree, Arizona Highways, Mid-America Review, Tamaqua, Dacotah Territory,* and many other publications. Bush has contributed to many literary anthologies, including *The First Skin Around Me; The Remembered Earth: An Anthology of Contemporary Native American Literature; Durable Breath: Contemporary Native American Poetry; Harper's 20th Century Native American Poetry;* and *Returning the Gift: Poetry and Prose from the First North American Native Writers' Festival.*

Bush has taught Native American literature at Milwaukee Area Technical College, New Mexico Highlands University, and Institute of the Southern Plains. He has been visiting writer for the state of North Carolina and the recipient of a number of grants by state arts councils and writer-in-resdency programs at universities. In 1995 he published a work of spoken poetry, released on compact disc, *A Sense of Journey,* from NATO Records in Paris, France.

In 1992, Bush delivered a plenary session speech at the historic Returning the Gift confer-

Barney Bush, a Shawnee and Cayuga, has published poetry in many publications and anthologies. He teaches at the Institute of American Indian Arts in Santa Fe, New Mexico.

NATO Records, Paris, France, produced *A Sense of Journey*, on CD, a volume of spoken poetry by Tony Hymas and Barney Bush. This is a poster advertising the recording to French-speaking listeners.

ence of North American Native literary writers at the University of Oklahoma. This conference drew nearly four hundred participants from throughout the northern half of the Western Hemisphere.

SEE ALSO:
Returning the Gift.

BUSHOTTER, GEORGE (1864–1892)

George Bushotter (Lakota), the first Lakota to write an account of his people in their own language, became known as "The First Lakota Ethnographer." He was born in 1864 in Dakota Territory (present-day North and South Dakota) near the confluence of the Moreau and Missouri Rivers. His parents, a Yankton father and a Minneconjou mother, called their son Oteri. Oteri, meaning "trouble," was brought up to follow the traditional Lakota way of life. As a child, he lost his father, who was killed by white men while the family was traveling along the Missouri River. His mother eventually remarried a man named Amos Goodroad from Lower Brule agency.

In 1878, Oteri traveled to Hampton, Virginia, as part of the first group of forty-nine Native students recruited from Dakota Territory by Richard Henry Pratt to attend the Hampton Normal and Agricultural Institute. At Hampton, the new student's name was recorded by school officials in English and Lakota and amalgamated into "Bushotter" by mistake. By the time the error was uncovered, the unique surname had become too fixed to alter. Bushotter remained at Hampton until 1881, when he returned home and served as an assistant teacher in the Lower Brule boarding school.

In 1882–1883, he escorted a group of newly recruited students to Hampton Institute, reenrolling in the school himself to continue his studies. In 1885, after a visit home, Bushotter enrolled in the Theological Seminary of Virginia to prepare for the ministry. However, he discontinued his theology studies on the advice of faculty, who found that his limited English skills hindered his study of other languages, an important part of theological studies. Bushotter then found employment

with the Reverend James Owen Dorsey, the Siouan scholar, at the Bureau of American Ethnology. During his ten-month tenure as an ethnographer, Bushotter provided Teton linguistic material, wrote stories and other texts in Lakota, and assisted in preparing language material later used in the *Handbook of American Indians North of Mexico*, edited by Frederick W. Hodge.

Bushotter's important Lakota writings provide a pioneering, firsthand account of his tribal culture. The original manuscript of this account is at the Smithsonian Institution in Washington, D.C. As of 1996, although two groups of scholars have been working on a translation, Bushotter's work remains unpublished.

Bushotter married Evalina Hull, a European-American woman he met while spending a summer in Hedgesville, West Virginia, working with Dorsey. Although he returned to Dakota Territory to teach in 1888, he resigned the following year. Bushotter, whose health continued to decline after a return east, died of tuberculosis in Hedgesville on February 2, 1892.

SEE ALSO:
Bureau of American Ethnology.

SUGGESTED READING:
Walker, James R. *Lakota Myth*. Lincoln: University of Nebraska Press, 1983.

BUTLER, DARRELLE (1942–)

Darrelle "Dino" Butler was born April 8, 1942, in Portland, Oregon. He is a member of the Confederated Tribes of Siletz and is also of Hupa, Yurok, Klamath, Pit River, and Yahooskin-Snake ancestry. He was raised mostly in logging camps in and around the Siletz reservation area in Oregon. Since 1974, Butler has been involved in a variety of spiritual and political activities. As a result of this work, he has been imprisoned in both the United States and Canada.

During the 1970s, Butler became involved with the American Indian Movement (AIM) and worked to establish a spiritual camp at Oglala, South Dakota. On June 26, 1975, an FBI attack on this camp resulted in the deaths of two FBI agents and one Native American. Butler was arrested and charged with murder for the deaths of the FBI agents. The 1976 trial, in which Butler was acquitted, drew national attention.

Later in the 1970s, Butler participated in the Minnesota Citizens' Review Committee on FBI misconduct, working toward the release of Leonard Peltier, a fellow Native American activist, who was convicted on state charges stemming from the 1975 incident at Oglala. In 1978, Butler participated in the Longest Walk, a trek from San Francisco to Washington, D.C., that drew hundreds of walkers and tens of thousands of participants in activities that took place along the way. The Longest Walk dramatized the grievances of Native people against anti-Indian legislation, policies, and actions, including the imprisonment of Peltier. In 1979, Butler sought political asylum, or refuge, in Canada, but the Canadian government denied his request because he had returned to the United States to testify as a defense witness in the Peltier trial.

In 1981, while in Canada to attend an indigenous spiritual ceremony, Butler was arrested and charged with weapons possession and attempted murder. While in custody at Oaklalla Prison in British Columbia, he contributed to the efforts of Native prisoners to gain religious freedom that set precedents in the corrections system. In January 1982, he completed a twenty-two-day spiritual fast with his codefendant and cousin, Gary Butler, for the right to hold sacred pipe ceremonies in the prison. That same month, at their trial in Westminster, B.C., the judge refused to allow the sacred pipe in the courtroom. In response, the Butlers refused to speak or participate in the trial. Because Butler's identity was based on the pipe, the court's demand that he be separated from his identity in this way was, in Butler's view, a way of saying that he was "nothing." In Butler's words, "I had been nothing for too long and I would not have my physical being separated from my spiritual being any longer." (The judge finally allowed the presence of the pipe in the courtroom in 1984, after Native religious rights had been established in other institutional settings.)

Despite the Butlers' refusal to participate in their own trial and the absence of defense lawyers in their case, they were found "not guilty" of attempted murder. They were, however, convict-

ed of weapons possession, for which they were sentenced to the maximum four-year penalty.

In 1983, Butler held another spiritual fast—this one for thirty-four days—resulting in the first sweat-lodge ceremonies ever held in Canadian prisons. Through his actions, Butler helped secure religious freedom not only for himself but for other Native prisoners in the Canadian corrections system.

In 1984, elders and hereditary chiefs of the Longhouse requested Butler's release to the Longhouse. Their request was denied, and Butler was deported to Newport, Oregon, to face charges for the murder of a well-known grave robber. He was acquitted of all charges in 1985.

Butler relocated to the Native American spiritual community of Redwind in central California in 1988. He lived there until his return to Siletz, Oregon, in 1992. His many years of commitment to Native people continue to this day. He is currently involved with Oregon Native Youth Council, a group of grassroots people working toward the restoration and preservation of traditional Native culture and values through spiritual reawakening, as well as the elimination of all kinds of oppression, especially institutional oppression, affecting Native youth and their families.

— E. K. Caldwell

SEE ALSO:

American Indian Movement; Longest Walk; Longhouse; Oregon; Peltier, Leonard.

CABEZA DE VACA, ALVAR NÚÑEZ (1490?–1557?)

Alvar Núñez Cabeza de Vaca, along with an African named Estevanico and two other Europeans, Andres Dorantes and Alonso del Castillo Maldonado, traveled on foot across much of the region that later became the American Southwest. Between 1528 and 1536, these men made their way from the Gulf coast of Texas to the Pacific Ocean near Culiacán, Mexico. Their account of this journey, especially of rumors they had heard of wealthy Indian civilizations in the north, inspired the Spanish to mount the expedition of Don Francisco Vásquez de Coronado in 1540, in search of fabled cities of gold.

The four men had left Spain in 1527 as members of a large colonizing expedition to northern Florida. There, finding themselves stranded, members of the expedition built rafts and attempted to sail westward across the Gulf of Mexico. They hoped to reach the Spaniards at the Mexican city of Tampico. Many died on the voyage. Of approximately one hundred men who made it to the Texas coast, only Cabeza de Vaca and the other three men mentioned above survived to ever reach other Spaniards. They did so by traveling on foot all the way across the continent. At times, they were taken as slaves by various tribes, and other times they were regarded as honored medicine men. They traveled across the southern Great Plains, reaching the Rio Grande River by the late summer of 1535. From there, they crossed into present-day Arizona and then turned southward. In March 1536, they startled a detachment of Spanish slave raiders under the command of Diego de Alcaraz, who escorted them to Culiacán. Accounts of their journey—and of the rumors of wealth that they had heard—soon reached the viceroy of Mexico, who immediately set into motion preparations that led to the Coronado expedition.

SEE ALSO:
Coronado Expedition; de Niza, Marcos; Spain.

CABOT, JOHN (c. 1450–c. 1499) AND SEBASTIAN (1476?–1557)

John Cabot, c. 1450–c. 1499, was an explorer who laid the groundwork for England's claim to the North American mainland. Born Giovanni Caboto in Italy, Cabot sailed for England, making the first English voyage to North America in 1497.

The exact date and place of Cabot's birth are not known. The archives of Venice, Italy, record that on March 28, 1476, he was accorded the rights of citizenship after fifteen years' required residence. By 1495, as Columbus was making his voyages to the "New World," Cabot was an English subject, living in Bristol with his wife, who also had emigrated to England from Venice. In 1496, Cabot and his heirs were commissioned by England's King Henry VII to search for land across the Atlantic

Ocean. The license issued by the king gave the Cabot family control over English commerce to and from any territories they might find, provided that one-fifth of all income ("the royal fifth") was turned over to the crown.

In May 1497, Cabot sailed west with a crew that may have included his son Sebastian. On June 24, Cabot sighted land: possibly what is now Newfoundland, Canada. Cabot's crew scouted the coast for several hundred miles but saw no people. They docked again at Bristol in August. The next year, the king authorized Cabot to hire six ships and crews, but this contract was never exercised. This agreement is the last record of Cabot's career. The exact time and place of his death are unknown.

Cabot's son Sebastian, who may have been born in 1476, continued to explore the "western seas" after his father's death, spurred by news of the voyages of Columbus. In May 1498, Sebastian Cabot led two ships from Bristol in search of a Northwest Passage through the Arctic Ocean to "the Indies," or Asia. The ships veered north into an area where summer daylight was almost continuous and the sea was filled with icebergs. Then, sailing southwest, the ships sighted Newfoundland. They followed the North American coast south to the area later named Chesapeake Bay (near present-day Delaware, Maryland, and Virginia). Along the coast, the explorers encountered several groups of Native people. Back in England, their expedition was regarded as a failure because they had not located a route to Asia.

After the death of his patron, Henry VII, in 1509, Sebastian Cabot was invited to sail under the Spanish flag by King Ferdinand V. In 1526, he sailed to South America and became the first European to sight the Río de la Plata. He also tried, and failed, to find a passage to Asia through what is now Argentina. He returned to Spain in 1530. In England, Edward VI assumed the throne in 1547 and issued a warrant for Cabot's return. Cabot, by now an elderly man, answered the summons in 1548, after which Edward VI restored John Cabot's original license to New World commerce. However, the value of the commission was never realized, and Sebastian Cabot died in 1557 in England.

SEE ALSO:
Columbus, Christopher.

A Bartolozzi engraving of a cacique of the island of Cuba addressing Christopher Columbus.

CACIQUE

The Spanish word *cacique* is a transformation of the Arawak word *kassequa*, meaning "chieftain." The first Spanish explorers noticed this title being used for the leaders of the Arawak, who greeted Christopher Columbus when he reached what we now know as San Salvador in the Bahamas.

Soon after contact in the Western Hemisphere, Spanish-speaking writers began to use *cacique* as a title for Indian chiefs or Indians of high rank. They began to call *caciques* those Indians they considered similar to lords or princes in their own country—that is, heads and rulers of tribes or districts.

For example, the writers of a travel book from 1577 report, "These Indians give great honor and reverence to their Cacique." Also, in his report about Hernando Cortés's march on the Aztec capital, Tenochtitlán, the soldier Bernal Díaz del Castillo uses the word *caciques* over and over: "The Caciques from all the neighboring towns"; "the Caciques and chief men"; "forty Indians arrived, all of the Caciques of good bearing, wearing rich mantles"; "a great Mexican Cacique."

Soon *cacique* was used in the Spanish-speaking West Indies, in South America, and Central America. Caciques often became minor judges who had to distribute the workload for the people and collect taxes for the Spanish. Much later, in post-colonial times, *cacique* was the title given to the bosses of labor gangs, for example in Mexico. Today, the word *cacique* and its derived form *caciquismo*, or bossism, has political meaning; it is used to designate the boss or local chief and the rule of local chiefs or bosses.

CADDO

Caddo is a contraction of *kadohadacho*, a word from the Caddoan language family that means "red chiefs."

Caddo villages were found by early non-Native explorers in what is now west-central Arkansas, where Caddo Gap and the Caddo River have received the Indian nation's name. The principal villages of the Caddo were located at the bend of the Red River in present-day southwestern Arkansas and northeastern Texas.

Chronicles of Hernando de Soto's expedition of 1541 refer to Caddos. It is also believed that Caddos made contact with Francisco Coronado.

Beef being distributed on the Wichita-Caddo Reservation, near Anadarko, Indian Territory, about 1900.

Zachary Taylor, a Caddo, in traditional dress of the early twentieth century in Indian Territory, at about the time the U.S. Congress was using allotment to erode the tribal land base.

feet. They were especially known for their friendly welcome to visitors, offering housing, food, and a place to clean up.

The Caddos were farmers, growing such crops as corn, beans, and pumpkins. They also mined salt, which they traded to other Indian nations before the coming of the Europeans. After the arrival of Europeans, the Caddos secured horses and became fine riders.

In the late 1700s, Caddo encampments north of the Red River were attacked by the Osage. Other southeastern nations also waged war against the Caddos in the 1700s.

After the Louisiana Purchase in 1803, it was reported that the Caddo Nation had suffered great losses among its people because of war and epidemics. Those Caddos who had aligned with the French then transferred their alliance to the United States. The Caddos and Choctaws joined together against their common enemy, the Osage.

In 1835, Caddo lands in Louisiana were ceded, and removal of the nation to Indian Territory—now Oklahoma—began. Some of the Caddo were living within the Choctaw Nation, and the Choctaws enacted legislation that all "intruders" must leave.

In the 1830s, the Caddos had been in possession of firearms for about one hundred years. As some Caddos moved farther into Texas, they—along with the Texas Cherokees—fell under suspicion and were forced to surrender their firearms.

However, there are no additional written references to the Caddos until the mid-1600s, when the Spaniards came into contact with the nation in Texas.

The Caddos were described by early non-Caddo writers as industrious, intelligent, sociable, and lively. They were small in stature but well built, robust, and strong. Caddo women were also described as pretty, with regular features and small hands and

In 1845, the Creek Nation in Indian Territory called for a great intertribal council, which some of the Caddo attended. At the council, Caddo Chief Chowawhana deplored the past and advised against hostility among the tribes.

Along with other Indian nations, the Caddos signed a treaty at Council Springs on the Brazos River in 1846. They acknowledged the United States as their protector and agreed to observe peace. The nations were given a land tract along the Brazos River consisting of 37,152 acres (148,608 hectares).

As they had in the past, the Caddos adapted to new conditions and lived peacefully. They planted their crops, fenced their fields, and erected houses. But colonizers were restless, and in other areas of the continent, Indian nations were at war with the U.S. government. Warriors and scouts from the Caddo Nation worked with the federal government on expeditions against other Indian nations.

After a group of whites attacked an encampment of Caddos, Texas officials decided to remove all the Brazos River nations to Indian Territory. The Caddos were forced to move in the August heat from their Brazos Reservation to an area near the Washita River.

During the U.S. Civil War (1861–1865), most Caddo groups sided with the Confederacy. The Caddo Battalion was one of the last Confederate Indian forces to surrender. Those who sided with the Union moved to Kansas. After the war, the Caddos returned to the Wichita-Caddo Reservation in Indian Territory.

With forced land allotments and the termination of Indian nation governments imposed on Native people by the U.S. government, the Caddos lost a considerable amount of their land. By 1901, their reservation had effectively been dissolved, but they reorganized under the Oklahoma Indian Welfare Act of 1936, with a corporate charter issued by the Secretary of the Interior. The Caddos established a constitution and bylaws and became known as the Caddo Indian Tribe of Oklahoma on January 17, 1938. They are headquartered near Binger, Oklahoma, and the council meets every month. Today, only about two-fifths of the Caddo people are full-bloods. The Caddos still practice the traditions of their culture within their communities.

In 1993, the Caddos were notified that museums across the country held artifacts and remains of their people. Caddos have sought to have the remains and artifacts returned to them and have discussed displaying the artifacts in a traveling museum so that the nation's members can view them.

— S. S. Davis

SEE ALSO:
Arkansas; Cherokee; Choctaw; Creek; de Soto, Hernando; Indian Territory; Louisiana Purchase; Osage; Texas.

SUGGESTED READINGS:
Debo, Angie. *A History of the Indians of the United States.* Norman: University of Oklahoma Press, 1970.
The World of the American Indian. Washington, D.C.: National Geographic Society.
Wright, Muriel H. *A Guide to the Indian Tribes of Oklahoma.* Norman: University of Oklahoma Press, 1951.

CAHOKIA

At its height, around 1100 or 1200 C.E., Cahokia was the largest center of Mississippian culture and the largest city north of Mexico. The city was about the same size as the largest urban centers in Europe, having a population of about ten thousand people. Cahokia is located six miles (about ten kilometers) from the Mississippi River, in what is today southern Illinois, not far from St. Louis, Missouri. The name *Cahokia* was given to a nearby town by the French, after a group of the Illini tribe living in the area, and later the name became attached to the mounds as well.

Cahokia was founded around 600 C.E. and grew in size and population over the next six hundred years. After about 1200, the population began a gradual decline, eventually dwindling to the size of a village. By 1500, the site had been completely abandoned.

At its height, the city encompassed an area of about 6 square miles (15.6 square kilometers) and contained 120 mounds. Some mounds were conical and were used for burials. Most, however, had flat tops that supported wooden buildings, or temples, which is a classic feature of Mississippian culture. The city had a large, central plaza that was surrounded by mounds and houses. The houses had pole frames plastered with clay and thatched roofs. A 300-acre (120-hectare) central area of the city, which contained the largest mounds, was enclosed by a wooden stockade, built around the year 1100. The stockade required fifteen thousand logs for its construction. Its walls rose to a height of 12 to 15 feet (3.6 to 4.5 meters), and it was rebuilt three times before the city was abandoned.

Cahokia contains the largest mound north of Mexico and one of the largest in the world. It has come to be called Monks Mound because French Trappist monks planted vegetable gardens and fruit trees on its terraces in the early nineteenth century. It has four terraces and reaches to a height of 100 feet (30.3 meters). Its base, a rectangle, measures 700 feet by 1,080 feet (212 meters by 328 meters).

At the summit of Monks Mound stood a large wooden building that measured 105 feet (32 meters) long, 48 feet (14.5 meters) wide, and 50 feet (15 meters) high. The base of Monks Mound covers more than 14 acres (5.6 hectares), which is an area larger than the base of the Great Pyramid of Egypt. The mound contains 22 million cubic feet (616,000 cubic meters) of dirt, all of which was moved one basketful at a time. The construction took three hundred years to complete, in fourteen distinct stages.

Despite its importance, Cahokia was studied only sporadically by archaeologists, many of them amateurs, while sustaining damage by modern, mechanized farming, until it was threatened by plans to construct Interstate Highway 255 through the site. Professional archaeologists, and others, rallied to save Cahokia from destruction, and they succeeded in getting a partial rerouting of the highway.

About half of Cahokia's 120 mounds survive, although most have been altered by farming, construction, and erosion. Excavations of some of the mounds have revealed a rich diversity of ornamental and functional artifacts. Trade was extensive over a large geographical expanse, bringing raw materials of shell, copper, mica, and other items to be fashioned into ornate objects.

An arrangement of red cedar posts in large circles was used to mark the seasons of the sun, especially the spring equinox, which is critically important data for agricultural communities. Crops such

Monks Mound, the largest mound in the city of Cahokia, has a base of more than 14 acres (5.6 hectares), larger than the Great Pyramid of Egypt. The city of Cahokia, in southern Illinois, not far from present-day St. Louis, Missouri, was abandoned by the year 1500.

as corn and squash were planted in the rich flood-plain of the Mississippi River. New strains of corn from Mexico that required a shorter growing season allowed people living in the area to harvest two crops of green corn and one crop of dried corn each year.

Excavations at Cahokia have revealed a high incidence of diseases resulting from urban crowding and poor sanitation, including tuberculosis, which is a contagious, deadly disease. In addition to such diseases, the death rate at Cahokia exceeded the birthrate. This was a characteristic of all cities, but it was especially high at Cahokia, making the maintenance of the population heavily dependent upon the immigration of people from rural areas. For some reason, possibly as a consequence of the unhealthy urban environment with its high mortality rate, people stopped moving to the city sometime around 1200, thus beginning the steady decline in population that would end in the city's abandonment by around 1500.

Only a few remnants of the mound-building culture survived to be described in detail by Europeans, including the Natchez of the lower Mississippi River valley. The Natchez survived for about a generation after the arrival of the French in the region.

— D. L. Birchfield

SEE ALSO:
Mississippian Culture; Mound Builders.

CALIFORNIA

California became the thirty-first U.S. state on September 9, 1850. Its name came from a story by the Spanish writer García Ordóñez de Montalvo, written in 1510, about an island of this name ruled by Black Amazons. Early Spanish explorers began using the fictional name to describe the area.

California has a long history of indigenous occupation, going back for at least twelve thousand years and perhaps, in the view of some scholars, for as long as thirty thousand years. The history of Native life in California is quite complex and varied. One must remember that there is no such thing as a single "Indian" culture. The terms Indian and Native American are used to refer to the hundreds of individual cultures that existed in the Americas at the time of European contact and that continue to flourish in this land. The "Indian history" of California is particularly complex and varied because nowhere else in the United States can one find so many Native cultures living side by side.

When Europeans first came to California, they found 200 to 300 Native cultures. They also learned that the Native peoples spoke over 150 different languages. Every one of the major Indian language families could be found in California. As waves of Indian migration passed through the area, some members of each group apparently decided to stay in California, until many Indian cultures existed side by side. The tribes included the Hupas, Yuroks, Pomos, Wishosks (Wiyots), Yukis, Yahis, and Maidus in the north; the Ohlones (Costanoans), Miwoks, Maidus, Salinans, and Yokuts in the center of the state; the Monos and Panamints in the east; and the Chumashes, Serranos, Diegueños, and Yumas in the south.

The California tribes had many distinctive talents. The Pomos developed basket weaving into an art, and Pomo baskets became so finely woven that they are sought by collectors. Some of the utility baskets are woven to hold water. The Chumashes, who lived near present-day Santa Barbara, made oceangoing vessels of pine planks lashed with animal sinew and made watertight with asphalt.

The first European expedition to California was led by Juan Rodríquez Cabrillo, who went to present-day San Diego in September of 1542. Sir Francis Drake explored the present-day area of San Francisco in 1579. The first European settlements were established in California in 1769 and 1770 when Captain Gaspar de Portola built forts at San Diego and Monterey. Spanish missions were built soon after the forts had been established. Twenty-one missions were built in California between 1769 and 1823. Thousands of California Indians were enslaved during the so-called mission period of Spanish occupation. Indians who resisted the system were flogged, imprisoned, tortured, and executed. As harsh as the mission period was, even more harsh times followed when California fell under U.S. control.

In 1849, when California was transferred by Mexico to the United States, one hundred thousand American Indians lived in the state. From 1850 through 1859, the U.S. government paid

Indian Grinding Rock, a site of the Konkou tribe in the North Sacramento Valley, near Oroville, California.

A Pomo feather basket.

California $924,259 for military campaigns against Native people, and by 1859, only thirty thousand Indians were left alive. Many government officials called for the complete eradication of all California Indians.

Somehow, many California Indians did manage to survive. Currently, California contains more reservations than any other state, 107 Indian reservations or recognized tribes in all. The 1990 U.S. Census lists 242,164 Indian people as California residents, placing California second among all states in Native American population. Los Angeles, with its 87,487 Indian residents, is the largest center of urban Indians in the country. However, only 17 percent of California's Indian population are Native people from tribes that are indigenous to California.

The great majority of Indians in California today have come from other parts of the continent. Of particular importance here were the federal relocation programs of the 1950s and 1960s, when the U.S. government attempted to terminate some Indian tribes by forcing their people to move to large urban centers, such as Los Angeles. The reloca-

tion programs were devastating to the tribes involved, but an unanticipated result has been a modern movement toward intertribalism. Relocated Native people in California from many different tribes have worked together for common political goals and to keep their cultural heritages alive.

Today, California Indians face many political and economic struggles. These include disputes over fishing rights and the operation of casinos and bingo games, as well as ongoing struggles concerning federal recognition and treaty rights. It is also a time of cultural revitalization. Many ceremonies and dances are being held throughout the state. These include such events as Big Times in central California and the performance of the Brush Dance, the Feather Dance, and the Jump Dance in northern California and the Bird Singers of southern California.

— T. Colonnese

SEE ALSO:
California Indians; California Missions; Mexico, Indigenous Peoples of.

A Pomo girl in traditional and contemporary dress.

CALIFORNIA INDIANS

Creation stories, which are often stories of a people's emergence from beneath the earth to its surface, reflect the worldview of Native peoples. The accounts are integrated into their ceremonies and are at the core of their identity. Such accounts provide a focus for the identity of Native people who are indigenous to California. These accounts lie behind the knowledge that California has long been populated by Native people, who date their beginnings to time immemorial—that is, to a time before human memory and written accounts could provide people with a record of human existence.

Out of the identity forged in their creation accounts, California Native peoples have also forged a deep connection to the land, a land that is large and varied. The area now known as the state of California is more than five hundred miles (eight hundred kilometers) in length and varies greatly in climate and terrain. The north coast is heavily forested and receives a lot of rainfall. The entire state becomes drier to the east and south. The central and south coasts are warmer, becoming hotter with fewer trees the farther south you go. The mountains in central California drop sharply to the east, where the land is mainly desert. The Colorado River forms the southeastern border of the state.

Thousands of years ago, the eastern desert areas of California were much wetter than they are today. Ancient lakes stretched for miles, and streams, marshes, and forests covered much of the current desert areas of the state. California was extremely rich with natural resources and supported a large number of tribes. The ancient inhabitants hunted. They collected the foods of the sea and lakes with fishing hooks, harpoons, and nets. They collected the foods of the land and marshes with snares and traps. They gathered eggs and wild grains, and they dried meat for the winter season. As far as hunting and gathering were concerned, California was one of the richest areas of North America.

The Indians of California developed complex and varied cultures. Members of the different tribes built many types of houses. The Pomo, Chemehuevi, and Chumash made beautiful and intricate baskets that are, today, valued worldwide. The cave paintings of the Chumash and their ancestors are thought to be some of the best ancient art in North

America. The Gabrielino and Chumash are known for their polished carvings and bowls made from soapstone, a smooth, soft type of rock. The Mohave are famous for their singing. Religious dreams are important to the Paiutes of California and Nevada. It was one such dream that led to the Ghost Dance religion, which was adopted by many North American Indian groups in the late 1800s.

Much is known about the long history of Indian occupation in California from Native oral traditions. Every year, archaeological investigations add to the scientific record. Trade was an important activity that put the region in contact with other areas of the continent, which promoted the exchange of ideas as well as goods. For example, there is archaeological evidence of trade in pottery between southern California coastal tribes and the Hohokam culture of the Southwest between 700 and 900 C.E. Turquoise mines were also started in the eastern desert during this period, and the gem soon became an important item of trade.

The Spanish explorer Juan Rodríguez Cabrillo landed his ship near what is today the city of Ventura on October 10, 1542. He was the first European to reach the coastal area of California. The Indian population declined following this first European contact. The causes of this decline included diseases, warfare, and enslavement by the Europeans.

When the Spanish mission system was set up in the 1770s, entire tribes were pulled into the missions for labor. Many of the tribes are named after the mission to which they were relocated. This relocation disrupted the traditional way of life of many tribes. However, many California Native people resisted the mission system by escaping into the interior, while others led revolts. Most of the ones who were forced into the mission system resisted in other ways. The mission system was meant to destroy Native culture and replace it with Christianity. Mission Indians kept their cultures alive by continuing to practice their traditional ceremonies. For example, the autobiography of Delfina Cuero describes a girl's puberty ceremony being performed, even though it was forbidden.

In 1812, the Russians built a colony at Fort Ross on the northern coast of California and began fur trading with the Indians. In 1821, California passed from Spanish to Mexican rule, and in 1834, the fifteen thousand Indians who had been enslaved in the missions were released. As a result, many of the Indians left the missions and ended up as laborers on the large farms, called *ranchos*.

The activity of American fur traders and whalers brought U.S. attention to Mexican-controlled California. The expedition of mountain man Jedediah Smith into California in 1826 eventually led to settlers entering the area by an overland route from the east in 1841. U.S. influence greatly increased in California from this time on until 1846, when the U.S. government gained control of the state during the Mexican War.

The Indians in California were now subjected to the U.S. national Indian policies. Under these policies, Indians were removed from land wanted by other Americans or forced to assimilate into the dominant Euro-American culture. Some of those policies led to the establishment of reservations in California.

The California gold rush of the late 1840s was a disaster for some of the smaller California tribes. Many simply disappeared during this period, and all of the tribes became smaller. A major reason for the decline of the California tribes during the gold-rush years was the ruthless killing of the Indians by white claim seekers. Although most Indians posed no threat to the mining activities, one forty-niner noted that whites slaughtered Indians "as they would wild beasts."

In the 1860s, the Modoc tribe was removed to a reservation in Oregon. Conditions became so bad there that they went home to their traditional land in northern California's Lassen County. The attempts by the U.S. Army to again move them to the Oregon reservation started the Modoc War. It took over 1,000 U.S. Army troops to defeat about 150 Modoc warriors, led by their chief, Captain Jack. After the Modoc defeat, many of the warriors were sent to Indian Territory (present-day Oklahoma) as prisoners of war. A few were sent to the military prison on the island of Alcatraz. This was the last Indian war of the nineteenth century in California.

By the 1870s, only scattered members of most of the tribes in California remained. Most lived on reservations, some of which were newly created for them. The Indians in California were no longer considered to be a serious threat to the occupation

Children visit the ceremony house at Indian Grinding Rock State Park, Volcano, California.

and exploitation of the state by non-Indians, but their usefulness as free labor continued under the bonded servant system. Through this system, young Indian people were kidnapped from the reservations and sold into service. This service continued until the individual worked long enough to earn freedom from bond. This system lasted in California up until the 1890s, some thirty years after the U.S. Civil War freed the Black slaves.

Under the provisions of the Dawes Allotment Act of 1887, the Bureau of Indian Affairs (BIA) began to break apart some of the reservation lands. This was known as allotment. The land was then distributed to individual Indians. In California, less than one-fourth of the reservation land was allotted, far less than in other places.

At the beginning of the twentieth century, most California Indians worked as general farm laborers, herdsmen, grain harvesters, fruit pickers, and servants. The work was often seasonal, and the wages were very low. A very few still tried to live according to their ancient, traditional lifestyle in the forests and mountains. Ishi, the last Yahi tribal member alive, finally abandoned his traditional way of life during this time and came out of hiding in 1911, after all of his people had been murdered.

In 1906, Congress started granting additional reservations for California Indians, and by 1930, thirty-six small *rancherias*, as these reservations were called, had been created. During World War I,

The Aqua Caliente Festival at Palm Springs, California.

many California Indians served as soldiers, fighting in Europe during 1917 and 1918. And like Native Americans in other parts of the country, California Natives did not become U.S. citizens until after the war was over, by the Indian Citizenship Act of 1924.

In the 1930s, many Indian people came to California during the Great Depression. Some came from Oklahoma, fleeing from the Dust Bowl. This disaster occurred because drought destroyed crops in the central-plains region and caused the loose

229

topsoil to blow away. The most common work to be found in California was low-paying seasonal labor on farms and in orchards picking fruit.

During the 1940s, many Indian people passed through California on their way to fight in the Pacific against the Japanese during World War II. Many California Indians served in the armed forces during this time or assisted with the war effort in shipyards and other war-related industries.

During the 1950s, under the Eisenhower Indian Relocation program, there was a massive migration of Native Americans from other states into California. Also, during this decade several Native American Urban Centers were started in California, like the American Indian Center in the Mission District of San Francisco. These centers were a home away from home for some relocated Indian people. In 1955, the BIA ended health and other services that had been guaranteed to California Indians by the U.S. government. In 1958, the U.S. Congress authorized the termination of California Indian tribes, and eventually the thirty-six rancherias were terminated.

In the 1960s, termination and relocation ended, and new federal assistance programs became available to California Indians, which helped to replace some of the services ended in the 1950s. During the 1960s, several organizations in California were started to provide other benefits. These included the Inter-Tribal Council of California and the California Rural Indian Health Program.

In 1964, Native Americans first attempted to occupy the government-owned island of Alcatraz. The island had basically been abandoned when the federal penitentiary was closed, and Native people felt that occupying this land would draw attention to many of their problems. The Indians were quickly removed by federal marshals.

In 1968, the U.S. Indian Civil Rights Act was passed by Congress, but changes were slow to come. Indians again occupied Alcatraz Island in the fall of 1969. This was politically significant for Native Americans nationally because it drew attention to the still much-needed civil rights reforms and to the arson fire that had destroyed the San Francisco American Indian Center. It was also historically significant because Alcatraz was the location of a military prison before the federal penitentiary was built there. Some of Captain Jack's warriors from the Modoc War were imprisoned there, as were Native Americans from California and other states.

During the 1970s, political protest helped publicize the loss of Native American cultural sites that had been brought about by non-Indians building on previously undeveloped land. These protests led to the passage of state laws to protect Indian heritage in California.

Throughout the 1980s and 1990s, California Indian housing, employment, and education have continued to improve. Traditional ways and language are beginning to make a comeback in many of the California tribes. Organizations like the American Indian Historical Society and the California Indian Education Association are involved in providing new teaching materials on Native American Californians to schools in the state. The National Native American AIDS prevention center has been educating Native Americans nationwide about the HIV/AIDS epidemic since the late 1980s. Many other Native American organizations are active in California universities and colleges throughout the state.

There are now eleven reservations and about seventy rancherias or smaller Indian landholdings in the state. The best-known reservation is the Agua Caliente Reservation, upon which half of the city of Palm Springs is built. Indian political action continues today in California as Indians fight illegal trash dumping on reservation land in the Mohave Desert. Because of the relocation program and a natural population increase, according to the 1990 U.S. Census California has the second-largest Native American population in the United States.

— J. D. Berry

SEE ALSO:

Alcatraz; Dawes Commission; Dust Bowl; General Allotment Act; Modoc War; Relocation Program.

SUGGESTED READINGS:

Heizer, Robert F. *The Natural World of the California Indians*. Berkeley: University of California Press, 1980.

Hurtado, Albert L. *Indian Survival on the California Frontier*. New Haven: Yale University Press, 1988.

Rawls, James J. *Indians of California: The Changing Image*. Norman: University of Oklahoma Press, 1984.

CALIFORNIA MISSIONS

The mission system was one of the three main institutions that the Spanish used to colonize new areas. The other two were *presidios* (or forts) and *pueblos* (or towns). The first Spanish mission in Alta California (today's state of California) was established in San Diego in 1769 by the Franciscan friar Junipero Serra. Serra would go on to establish eight more missions, and by 1823, when the last mission was established in San Francisco, the Franciscans had twenty-one missions stretched along southern and central California.

For Spain, the missions in California served a dual purpose. Of primary concern to the Spanish Crown was the protection of California from incursions by the English and Russians who were becoming much more active in the Pacific because of the lucrative sea otter trade. Spain had long claimed California by "right of discovery" but had failed to protect its claim by colonizing this very remote region. This colonization effort began in earnest with the establishment of the first mission and continued into the era of Mexican independence.

In addition, the Spanish Crown and the Catholic Church were interested in converting the Native populations of California to Christianity. The crown needed loyal subjects, especially in underpopulated areas, and the church's concern was to obtain converts to Catholicism.

The mission system in California served both the purposes of the crown and the church and was the primary tool for colonization by the Spanish. By congregating Indian populations around a mission, the Spanish gained control of both the Native inhabitants and their land. The Native people were regarded as a ready supply of labor for the Spanish colonists and for the missions themselves. They were taught to farm nonindigenous crops and to herd domesticated animals, such as cattle and sheep. They were taught trades like carpentry, tanning, and masonry in order to build and sustain the missions. The original Californians were forced to give up their way of life and to renounce their own spirituality in favor of Christianity in the form of Roman Catholicism.

The mission system was devastating to the Native populations of California. It represented an attempt to completely transform the culture and worldview of these people. The Spanish encountered several different Indian groups, including the Chumash, Luiseno, Kumeyaay (Diegueño), Salinan, Miwok, and others whose tribal economies were based on hunting, fishing, and the gathering of food resources from their environment. The missionaries used corporal punishment and other means of social control in their quest to transform the Native Californians into some form of Spanish peasantry. At the time of the arrival of the Spanish, California's Native population numbered approximately 310,000 to one million. When the mission system dissolved in 1834, that number had declined to some 98,000. The decline can be directly attributed to the harsh living conditions and the spread of European diseases among the congregated Native people.

The California Natives did not submit willingly to this attempt to conquer them. Initial efforts to establish missions were met with resistance. Even with the Spanish superiority in weapons, they were unable to prevent the burning of the San Diego mission in 1775, the near destruction of the San Gabriel mission in 1785, and the partial destruction of the Santa Ines mission in 1824. The Natives also resisted the mission system by taking flight from the missions in large numbers. This tactic served to decrease the labor supply at the missions and increase the level of resistance among Indians not already under control of the mission system.

The California mission system ended in 1834 when Mexican authorities secularized the missions—that is, they removed their religious emphasis, in effect freeing the Natives. The irony is that the mission Indians had few places to go. In many cases, they were given plots of mission land only to be swindled out of it by unscrupulous citizens. By this time, Indian villages had been replaced by towns, and missions had been transformed into Mexican ranches. Many of the mission Indians had no choice but to become laborers on the Mexican ranches following the end of the mission system in California.

— M. A. Stout

SEE ALSO:

California; California Indians; Catholic Church in the Spanish Empire.

Carmel Mission, California, was constructed by the Spanish in 1770.

CALUMET PIPE AND DANCE

The Calumet Dance was a specific ceremony for people who participated in a smoking ritual with the calumet pipe, a ceremonial smoking instrument of American Indians. Many tribes throughout the Americas celebrated significant events in their lives by smoking this highly ornamented pipe. After placing tobacco in the bowl of the pipe stem, many Indian people took turns taking puffs from the pipe with the intent of cleansing their body and mind. This would heighten the clarity of their thoughts during healing sessions, meetings, conferences, or conflict mediation. In smoking the calumet pipe, straight posture, dignity, and a sincere effort to listen to one's inner voice was extremely important. Respect was bestowed upon each person who participated in the ceremony.

The pipe was usually the length of an adult's arm, with the shaft constructed of wood and the bowl carved from dark red pipestone rock. The only natural location in the country from which the pipestone can be retrieved legally is in Pipestone, Minnesota. The Dakota of Minnesota are careful to monitor these sacred stones as they continue to respect and celebrate the sacred pipestone in traditional ways.

Indian people were careful to follow their unwritten code of rules when smoking the pipe. This code was part of a larger group of tribal rules that established tribal customs and helped develop the rules for responsible adult behavior. Usually, a trustworthy person, called the "pipe carrier," would be in charge of taking great care of the calumet pipe.

The Calumet Dance is most popular among the Plains Indians, although there are many versions of the dance as it is enacted by other Indian people. Most customs of the Calumet Dance were transmitted through oral tradition and learned through repetition and rote memorization. Usually, tribal songs were composed to explain the significance of the smoking ritual. Singers would beat with sticks on drums made of deerskin or cowhide, usually suspended from a frame to enhance the sound. Drum sticks were long enough to reach the center of a large, round drum from a sitting position. This permitted eight to twelve seated men to encircle the drum and sing in harmony, while beating the drum in unison all at the same time. In this context, the term *drum* can mean both the instrument and the group of singers. Gifts are customarily presented to the drum and participants in the dance. The drum returns its thanks with a vigorous "drum roll."

SEE ALSO:
Dance, American Indian.

CAMP GRANT MASSACRE

On April 30, 1871, a group of armed civilians from the town of Tucson, in the Territory of Arizona, led an expedition to the Apache rancheria near Camp Grant, Arizona. Under cover of night, all of the Apaches were slaughtered while they slept. To this day, the death count is unknown, but historians suspect that during the Camp Grant Massacre the attackers killed more than one hundred Apaches, primarily women, children, and elderly people.

The months preceding the massacre had been full of tension for Indians and non-Indians in the region. The rapid occupation of the area by non-Indians squeezed the Apaches out of their homeland, making it impossible for them to manage the resources of the land in their traditional manner. The Apaches responded by regarding the white settlements as a source of food, clothing, weapons, and livestock. Apaches also attacked the mines, mail coaches, and stagecoaches of the invading white colonizers. The Apaches were also reported to have run raids against the Tohono O'odham, a farming tribe located in the Tucson area. As the Apaches defended the invasion of their homeland, local newspapers began to fan the flames of fear and hostility toward the Apaches, calling for their annihilation.

A confusing national policy toward the Indians aggravated the situation. The citizens of the Arizona Territory had petitioned the commander in chief of the territory for additional protection against the Apaches. This request was denied, and indeed, many of the existing military posts in the region were disbanded.

At the same time, the military commander of Camp Grant, Lieutenant Royal Whitman, was holding peace talks with the Apache leader Eskiminzin. Whitman encouraged Eskiminzin to bring his band to Camp Grant to live in peace in return for government rations. Eventually, some five hundred people of the Arivaipa and Pinal bands of Apaches moved near Camp Grant, establishing a settlement that was referred to as a rancheria. Although their status was officially that of prisoners of war, the Apaches were not confined nor were their weapons confiscated. Whitman wrote to his superiors, asking for direction in handling this situation, but he received no answer. His requests for additional supplies to help feed the Apaches were likewise not answered.

Meanwhile, hostilities continued in the Tucson area after Eskiminzin's bands of Apaches relocated to the Camp Grant rancheria. Local newspapers published evidence that the resistance was being waged by the Apaches from Camp Grant. The local citizens became outraged. They were convinced they were being attacked by Apaches who were under the protection of the U.S. military.

Mass meetings with the intention of forming a citizen's militia to fight against the Apaches were held in Tucson. For several months, there was a lot of inflammatory talk but no action. Finally, a couple of men decided to take matters into their own hands. They secretly planned an expedition to kill the Apaches at Camp Grant. Jesus Elias led a group of volunteers, including ninety-four Tohono O'odham Indians, forty-eight Mexicans, and six white settlers on the April 30 attack.

The massacre of the Apaches at Camp Grant sparked outrage among politicians, the press, and the public back East. The Tucson government was ordered to prosecute those responsible for the massacre. But whites in the area felt the massacre was justified, and a local grand jury only indicted the perpetrators after threat of a military trial if no civil trial was held. After the grand jury passed down 108 indictments for murder, it was decided that a single member of the Camp Grant expedition, Sidney DeLong, would stand trial for the group. If he were convicted, all members of the expedition would be convicted. If he were acquitted, so would they be. The prosecution presented clear evidence that the members of the Camp Grant expedition massacred the Apaches. The defense was based on a justification of the massacre, presenting evidence that Apache resistance was waged by Eskiminzin's band.

After a long, involved trial, DeLong was acquitted by the jury after only nineteen minutes of deliberation. There was no further legal action taken against the men who massacred the Apaches at Camp Grant.

— M. A. Stout

SEE ALSO:
Apache.

CAMP VERDE RESERVATION

Camp Verde Reservation, approximately five hundred acres (two hundred hectares) in central Arizona, is the home of the Yavapai-Apaches. Tribal headquarters are at Camp Verde, Arizona. The Camp Verde Apaches have the highest percentage of their students enrolled in college of any tribe in Arizona. Divided into several small fragments, the reservation is shared by about an equal number of Tonto Apaches and Yavapai living in three communities—Camp Verde, Middle Verde, and Clarksdale. About half of the twelve hundred tribal members live on the reservation.

The original tract of 40 acres (16 hectares), acquired in 1910, is at Camp Verde. By 1916, an additional 400 acres (160 hectares) had been added at Middle Verde. Middle Verde is the seat of government, where a tribal council elected from the three communities convenes. About 280 acres (112 hectares) at Middle Verde are suitable for agriculture.

In 1969, sixty acres (twenty-four hectares) were acquired at Clarksdale, a donation of the Phelps-Dodge Company when it closed its Clarksdale mining operation. This land was to be used as a permanent base for the Yavapai-Apache community that had worked in the Clarksdale copper mines. An additional seventy-five acres (thirty hectares) of tribal lands surround the Montezuma Castle National Monument.

For the Yavapai-Apache, with its small amount of land suitable for agriculture, the tourist complex at the Montezuma Castle National Monument is an important source of employment and revenue. The monument contains some of the most spectacular cliff dwellings in the Southwest, constructed by people of the Sinagua culture before the arrival of Europeans.

Tonto Apaches and Yavapai-Apaches from Camp Verde perform public dances each year at the Coconino Center for the Arts, Flagstaff, Arizona, during the Fourth of July. The Yavapai-Apaches occasionally present public performances of the Mountain Spirit Dance. The Mountain Spirit Dance, or Crown Dance, as it is sometimes called, is a masked dance in which the participants impersonate deities of the mountains. The Apache Fire Dance is also a masked dance.

Instruments for making music include the water drum, the handheld rattle, and the human voice. Another traditional instrument still used in ritual and ceremonial events is the bull roarer, a thin piece of wood suspended from a string and swung in a circle.

Not all dances are open to the public. Visitors should call the tribal office to find out when dances are scheduled at which they will be welcome.

SEE ALSO:
Apache; Sinagua; Yavapai.

CAMPBELL, BEN NIGHTHORSE (1933–)

Ben Nighthorse Campbell, U.S. Senator, was born in Auburn, California, on April 13, 1933. Campbell is Cheyenne and is considered by many as a strong advocate of Indian rights within the U.S. government.

Campbell received his bachelor's degree at the University of California at San Jose. He then became an educator in a Sacramento, California, law enforcement agency. From 1983 to 1986, he was a member of the Colorado General Assembly. He was named Outstanding Legislator by the Colorado Bankers Association in 1984 and was the 1984 Man of the Year for the LaPlata Farm Bureau in Durango, Colorado. Campbell was named one of the ten best legislators by the *Denver Post* and Channel 4 TV in Denver in 1986.

In 1987, Campbell was elected from Colorado to the U.S. House of Representatives, where he remained active in Native American issues. He

Ben Nighthorse Campbell (second from right), U.S. Senator from Colorado, is a member of the Cheyenne Nation.

was elected to the U.S. Senate in 1992 as a Democrat, but in 1995, he changed his party affiliation to Republican.

Campbell is a member of the American Quarter Horse Association, the Aircraft Owners and Pilots Association, the American Brangus Association, and the American Indian Education Association. He is also an avid motorcyclist and a rancher in Ignacio, Colorado. He is also a jewelry designer, and many of his works are sold throughout the United States through catalogs.

A number of Campbell's legislative actions have been controversial among Native American people. He voted for NAFTA (North American Free Trade Agreement), legislation that fails to recognize the sovereignty of Indian nations in North America. He voted to keep national monuments open to off-road vehicles. He led the fight for legislation to restrict the term *Indian artist* to only federally recognized U.S. Indian artists, which excludes Canadian and Mexican Natives, all members of federally terminated tribes, and many East Coast Indians. Critics say the bill was supported by a small group of Santa Fe, New Mexico, area Native artists as a way of reducing competition.

CANADA, NATIVE–NON-NATIVE RELATIONS IN

British trade contact with the aboriginal, or Native, nations living in what is today Canada began after 1497 when English fish merchants began friendly trade with the aboriginal nations on the East Coast of North America.

French trade with aboriginal nations began when French merchants reached Hochelaga (now Montreal) and established posts there and on Newfoundland and Cape Breton. Quebec, which was founded in 1608, became known as Canada. Because the French presence in North America was based primarily on establishing centers of trade and mercantile exchange, French settlers were overwhelmingly male. The French established trade relations with the Algonquians and the Huron Confederacy and lived with them to become *couriers de bois*—good woodsmen and trappers who traveled and traded freely among their Native partners.

Divided Allegiances
The French were, however, hostile to the Iroquois, who were trade friends of the English. The Iro-

This engraving depicts a station of the Hudson's Bay Company in the Canadian Northwest.

quois, a sophisticated government of five united nations, included the Mohawks, Oneidas, Cayugas, Senecas, and Onondagas. Their alliance with the English represented a huge territory on the East Coast of North America.

As relations between Native people and French settlers became increasingly friendly, French law prohibited French people in Canada from living with the Natives. Rather than encourage French settlers to keep away from Native people, however, this effectively forced the settlers to escape the control of the government of France and give up their loyalty to their mother country.

These Frenchmen—the *couriers de bois* who lived, traveled, and traded freely among Native people—came increasingly to live with and marry Native people. The mixed-blood descendants of these French and Native people became known as Métis. They traded with Albany, a Dutch trading post founded in 1609 by Henry Hudson on what is today called the Hudson River. This post was later turned over to the British and named New York.

The Hudson's Bay Company obtained exclusive trade rights from Britain in 1670 in all lands that could be reached from the Strait of Hudson Bay. English trade posts around Hudson Bay became a point of trade with the Cree and other nations. The marriages between Natives and French *couriers de bois*, as well as their Métis offspring, became an important link to Native Canada for the British, who were eager to move westward to establish more trade posts.

In 1663, Canada had become a French Royal Colony. In 1669, an edict brought women from France to keep the Frenchmen loyal. The French in Canada grew quickly and spread out. In 1671, the French claimed the trade area from Sault St. Marie (in southern Ontario opposite the Upper Peninsula of Michigan) to the Pacific, and trade posts were set up. The French in Canada began to enter territory claimed by the Hudson's Bay Company for trade. Wars broke out between the French and the Iroquois around Lake Superior. The Iroquois attacked French posts, and the French raided the Iroquois in what is now New York state.

The French made friends with the Illinois peoples to establish their trade presence in the Mississippi Valley. The French also sought to use their relationship with the Illinois to halt the Iroquois, who were setting up new trade relations with the Northern Algonquians, who in turn had access to the English Hudson Bay trade posts in the north.

The Iroquois held trade control over the region, and all trade went to the English, who supplied them with guns and cheaper goods. A formal alliance between the English and the Iroquois Confederacy was sealed at Albany in 1684. Lord Howard Essingham, Governor General of Virginia, spoke of a covenant "strong and lasting even to the world's end." The Iroquois territory became a battle zone between the French and the English colonies as the French, with their Algonquian allies, sent raiding parties into English settlements in New England, New York, Schenectady, and Salmon Falls.

Resisting the British

Under the Treaty of Utrecht in 1713, the Hudson Bay trade region was awarded to the British to settle war debts in Europe between France and Britain. France had to release claims to Newfoundland and recognize British peace with the Iroquois Confederacy. France also had to hand over its settlements at Acadia (present-day Nova Scotia) to the English.

The Micmacs resisted strongly the shift of land and power to Britain, and they were armed with weapons and ammunition from the French naval base that had remained at Louisburg on Cape Breton Island in Acadi. For almost fifty years, the Micmacs fought the English with the urging of the French Acadians, who had lived side by side and intermarried with the Micmacs. Over the course of their conflict, Micmacs captured eighty English trading and fishing boats.

In 1744, war again broke out in Europe between England and France. In 1745, the English colonies raised a military force, waged war on the French naval base at Louisburg, and eventually captured Louisburg from the French. In 1749, the Micmacs formally declared war on the English, and the English governor issued a proclamation encouraging colonists to "destroy the Savages community called the Micmacs, wherever they are found." To urge English colonists to heed the call, the British paid them for Micmac scalps.

On July 15, 1977, at Blackfoot Crossing, Alberta, Canada, Prince Charles of Great Britain smokes a peace pipe with medicine man Ben Calfrope during a reenactment of the ceremony of the signing of Treaty 7 that took place here in 1877 with Queen Victoria and the Blackfeet Confederacy. The reservation is some 70 miles (113 kilometers) east of Calgary.

The Micmacs stopped their attacks after the English captured French Acadian military garrisons and, because the Acadians refused to swear their allegiance to Britain, deported them from Nova Scotia to English colonies in what is today the southern United States. Mistreated and in some cases enslaved by the English colonists, most of the deportees to the southern colonies died. Some of the Acadians made it to Quebec and some to the two small islands off Newfoundland that still belonged to France. Some twenty-five hundred French and Métis Acadians made it to the swamplands of Louisiana. Their descendants—known as Cajuns (from "Acadians")—today number around one million.

On the island of Newfoundland, the Beothuk were pushed away from their only food source, the sea. Over the next hundred years their numbers decreased as they died from illness and starvation or were killed outright by Europeans. Neither the English nor the French needed the Beothuk as allies, so they were never armed or made trading partners. In 1829, the last known Beothuk died, a servant in the household of an English justice of the peace.

When Louisburg fell to the British, it ceased to function as a naval supply base for the French. The British were able to shoot at will at French supply ships, and as a result the French were unable to support their Native allies in the Great Lakes region. Without a supply of guns and ammunition from the French, France's Great Lakes allies weren't nearly as friendly. In 1747, the Wyandots and Algonquians became openly hostile toward the French, further weakening France's power in North America.

In 1754, the governor of Virginia received orders to wipe out French rule in North America. A small number of troops under George Washington, with their Iroquois allies, were sent to expel the French. French troops and allies attacked and defeated Washington's troops, bringing other allies of the French back into line.

Full war between 1755 and 1763, which England called the French and Indian War, broke out between the French in Canada and their allies on one side and the English colonies and their allies on the other. English colonists brought in British troops to help in the war and gained the upper hand. In 1759, the English and their allies beat the French on the Plains of Abraham near the stronghold of Quebec. In 1760, Canada passed into British hands.

Following the surrender of the French to Britain, France's Great Lakes allies continued to resist the British, who were less civil than the French in their dealings with Native people. The French had made yearly gift payments for their use of Native lands. Unlike the French, however, the English made only one payment in their treaties to purchase lands around the colonies on the East Coast. England figured that by defeating the French, it now had ownership of the lands in which the French had traded and thus refused to make yearly payments.

In 1763, Chief Pontiac of the Ottawa organized a large allied force to oppose the British. They captured every British fort west of the Niagara except Detroit, effectively halting fur trade in the area. As their supplies of ammunition ran out, Pontiac's allied forces began trading with enemy English forts. As a way to stop further Native resistance, the English, that fall, at Fort Pitt (present-day Pittsburgh), gave the Indians a "present" of two blankets and a handkerchief from the fort's smallpox ward. The results were an epidemic, and slowly Pontiac's confederacy began to weaken as the English fought continuously over the next year to keep their trade routes open.

The British Seek Peace with Aboriginal Nations

The resistance of Native people to the British weakened both fur trade in the region and the economy of Britain. Pontiac's courageous revolt had made a peaceful plan necessary for the British, and the British Board of Trade and Plantations in London made plans to appease the aboriginal nations. At the urging of the Board of Trade, the Royal Proclamation of 1763 was passed. The proclamation became the legal tool that bound the old English colonies and the new colony of Canada in creating agreements in territories now under British domain.

The proclamation set aside a huge reserve west of the Allegheny Mountains for Native peoples with whom the colonies were allied. In the interest of peaceful trade, Britain agreed in the proclamation that it had no right to colonize without the consent of any tribe west of the heads of all the rivers that flowed into the Atlantic. Furthermore, this consent had to be obtained through a treaty.

Nellie Cournoyea, an Inuit and a Native rights' leader, drives a boat across Great Slave Lake in Yellowknife, the capital city of the Northwest Territories in northern Canada.

A Cree camp in the Canadian bush country of Quebec.

After the surrender of the French in Canada to Britain, the Quebec Act in 1774 confirmed the terms of surrender. Its main intent was to win the friendship of the British Canada's new "French Canadien" subjects. The act set out to establish the "province" of Quebec and allocated the region between the Ohio and the Mississippi Rivers, where some French had settled, for further expansion. This part of the Quebec Act was also designed to stop merchants of the old English colonies—those that lay along the East Coast of what would become the United States—from moving westward to gain trade.

The Quebec Act kept Britain's control of all merchant trade on land and sea and laid heavy taxes on the English colonies to pay for the war effort. This enraged the old colonies, which had begun to break their trade ties with Britain, and the idea of self-rule grew stronger in resistance to the Quebec Act. In 1775, the old colonists invaded Canada without making any real gains or doing serious damage to Canada. But the "American" revolution, followed in 1776 by the Declaration of Independence, in which the old colonists declared their independence from Britain, would become official.

After the War of Independence

In 1783, the Treaty of Paris ended the struggle between Britain and its American colonists. It recognized the independence of the American colonies and gave protection to British Empire loyalists wishing to leave the old colonies. It established a clear boundary between Canada and the United States on land and in the North Atlantic. But the Americans refused to abide by the provisions of the Proclamation of 1763, which would have defined boundaries separating the territory of the United States from the lands of the aboriginal nations and tribes to the west.

During the War of Independence, the British had taken great care to keep the friendship of their aboriginal allies and the "French Canadien" allies by giving both groups "presents" and high payment for furs. After the war, several thousand Iroquoian loyalists moved to Upper Canada. These were mostly Mohawks, Cayugas, and Onondagas who had fought for Britain. The British moved quickly to help them settle on reserves of their choosing. In the years directly following, the British supported aboriginal nations' claims in every dispute with American settlers in territories west of the Alleghenies.

The Americans settled the "Indian problem" by taking up war against Native nations, seizing their lands and forcing the British to give up their forts in the upper Mississippi Valley. There would soon be reason for war again between Americans and British. The Americans wanted to drive Britain from the whole of North America and carry out what it had failed to do in 1775.

In 1812, war was declared by the United States of America. The English lost their forts in Canada across Lake Erie. The Americans killed Tecumseh, who had led the aboriginal allies and gained control of the Michigan territory. York (present-day Toronto), the capital of Upper Canada, was also assaulted by U.S. forces. The Americans were driven back south as British forces arrived from England. In 1814, the British navy gained control of the whole East Coast to Maine and had captured Washington, the capital of the United States. After U.S. forces suffered an attack on Baltimore, fighting stopped and talking began.

In 1814, the Treaty of Ghent was signed between Britain and the United States. This treaty set forth a return to the way things had been before the war, instead of giving over captured U.S. posts to Britain. The Treaty of Ghent carried forward the principle of Jay's Treaty (the Treaty of Amnesty and Commerce of 1794) to maintain trade between Canada and the United States. The Treaty of Ghent also bound both countries to make peace with and provide free passage to the aboriginal peoples of North America.

The Rise of the Métis

Trade outposts west along the Great Lakes gave rise to a large population of mixed-blood Métis, who were at the front of the move westward as guides and traders through intermarriages. Their settlements expanded from the Upper Great Lakes to the Red River Valley and south through the Great Plains to the Arkansas River.

At the place where the Red and the Assiniboine Rivers meet (now Winnipeg), the Métis made large farming settlements and organized large armed units for hunting buffalo. They were allied with the Crees, with whom they had blood ties. They sold furs and buffalo meat to colonists. From the 1850s, the Métis colony grew and spread out. They made long trade trips to St. Paul in the United States. By the 1860s, they were powerful and wealthy.

In 1869, the Hudson's Bay Company turned over its trade rights in the area to Britain in exchange for a settlement colony. The French-speaking Métis refused to accept English control. They set up a Métis government with Louis Riel as their leader. The threatened loss of their lands and trade with the United States was an assault on the rights that came to them through their own hard work and from their Cree bloodlines. Riel's government set up a roadblock along the Red River road south of Fort Garry (Winnipeg), stopped the new British governor from entering Métis lands, and seized Fort Garry. Riel convened both the English-speaking population and the French-speaking Métis in a council to represent the whole colony. The goal of this council was to convince Britain and Ottawa to recognize the Métis government.

Britain and Ottawa agreed to Métis self-rule, thereby protecting Métis customs and lands in the new colony of Manitoba. The terms of agreement did not give amnesty to Riel or his followers, however. The execution of an Anglo Protestant from Ontario, who had worked against Riel, sparked racial and religious bitterness in Ottawa toward the French Catholic Métis. Using racial tension as an excuse, Canada sent a British and Canadian military force in 1870 to the Red River, even though self-rule had been granted to the Métis. The violence the Ontario militia exercised against Riel's people ended in great losses. To save his life, Riel fled into exile in the United States.

A Continuing Obligation to the Aboriginal Nations

The U.S. Civil War, during which Britain supported the Confederacy against the Union, had created among many Americans an anti-British feeling toward Canada, and U.S. gold miners were moving into the interior of British Columbia, which was just becoming established as a British colony on the West Coast. With fear of a U.S. takeover, the British North America Act was passed in 1867 by Britain's parliament, joining British North America into one federated unit called Canada. A central federal power over the provinces was the result of this federation, with the ties of that central power leading to Britain's parliament.

Section 91-24 of the British North America Act identified the federal government of Canada as the jurisdiction to watch over the crown's relationship with "Indians" and "Indian" lands. *Indian* was a generic term for aboriginal peoples, adopted from the U.S. practice of grouping separate aboriginal nations under one policy.

In 1870, the Manitoba Act granted provincial government status to what is today Manitoba under the Canada Constitution. The Manitoba Act transferred what was known as the District of Assiniboia into the new province. The remainder of the West was to be administered as the Northwest Territories under an appointed governor and council. An amendment in 1871 also gave the Dominion of Canada the right to create new provinces and decide their terms of entry.

Fifteen years after the first Riel uprising, the Métis and their Cree allies, led by Poundmaker and Big Bear, were in open rebellion against Canada as Cree and Métis lands were stolen and a law was passed against harvesting buffalo by any Métis. Louis Riel returned to Canada from the United States, and war broke out. Riel was defeated and executed for treason. The Red River was then thrown open to settlers without regard for the rights of the Métis.

Treaties with Britain under the Royal Proclamation in the Great Plains continued after confederation in 1867. These numbered treaties reserved lands for the exclusive use of aboriginal nations in what is now Manitoba, Saskatchewan, Alberta, and a part of northeastern British Columbia and surrendered lands to the crown in return for yearly guaranteed benefits.

As of 1982, when Canada was granted the right to form a new constitution, neither Britain nor Canada had yet completed treaties with the aboriginal nations in the rest of British Columbia, the Northwest Territories, the Yukon, Labrador, and parts of Quebec. The obligation Britain has to the aboriginal nations is guaranteed in Section 35 of the New Canada Act, which says Canada must "recognize existing treaty and aboriginal rights."

Through its passage of the Indian Act, Canada has chosen to interpret its duty to "Indians" to mean that it has authority over them and their lands and is attempting to redefine the relationship as this in its new constitution. However, as many aboriginal people and their advocates argue, in addition to being a sovereign nation, Canada remains an act of Britain's parliament in its obligations to the aboriginal nations. Without the consent of these nations, Canada cannot on its own redefine what is already recognized in the Canada Act of 1982.

— J. Armstrong

SEE ALSO:
Bill C-31; Hudson's Bay Company; Iroquois Confederacy; James Bay Hydro-Electric Project; Métis; Riel, Louis.

SUGGESTED READINGS:
Dickason, Olive Patricia. *Canada's First Nations: A History of Founding Peoples from Earliest Times.* Norman: University of Oklahoma Press, 1992.
Francis, R. I. Douglas. *Origins: Canadian History to Confederation.* Toronto: Coles Publishing Company, 1988.
Colden, Cadwallader. *The History of the Five Indian Nations of Canada.* Toronto: Coles Publishing Company, 1972.
Morton, W. L. *The Kingdom of Canada: A General History of Earliest Times.* Toronto: McClelland and Stewart Ltd., 1963.
McInnis, Edgar. *Canada: A Political and Social History,* 4th edition, with a final chapter by Michael Horn. Toronto: Holt, Reinhart and Winston of Canada, Ltd., 1982.

CANASSATEGO (c. 1690–1750)

Canassatego of the Onondaga was Tadadaho (speaker) of the Iroquois Confederacy in the mid-eighteenth century and a major figure in diplomacy with the French and English colonists. His advice that the colonies form a union on the Iroquois model influenced the plans for colonial union proposed by Benjamin Franklin as early as 1754. Later, a fictional Canassatego became a figure in English literature.

In 1744, Pennsylvania officials met with Iroquois sachems (chiefs) in council at Lancaster, Pennsylvania. This meeting was one of a number of significant diplomatic discussions involving English colonists, the Iroquois, and their allies that preceded, and helped shape the outcome of, the French and Indian War.

At the meeting, Canassatego and other Iroquois complained that the colonies, with no central authority, had been unable to restrain invasion of Native lands by white settlers. In that context, Canassatego advised the colonists to form a union emulating that of the Iroquois: "Our wise forefathers established Union and Amity [friendship] between the Five Nations. This has made us formidable; this has given us great Weight and Authority with our neighboring Nations. We are a powerful Confederacy; *and by your observing the same methods, our wise forefathers have taken* [emphasis added], you will acquire such Strength and power. Therefore whatever befalls you, never fall out with one another."

Richard Peters of Pennsylvania described Canassatego as "a tall, well-made man," with "a very full chest and brawny limbs, a manly countenance [expression], with a good-natired [sic] smile. He was about 60 years of age, very active, strong, and had a surprising liveliness in his speech."

At the time of the Lancaster council, Benjamin Franklin was in the midst of publishing the transcripts of Indian treaty councils as small booklets, which enjoyed a lively sale in the colonies and in England. The account of the Lancaster council was one of several dozen that he published between 1736 and 1762. Influenced by Canassatego's words at Lancaster, Franklin urged the English colonies to unite like the Iroquois Confederacy in a letter to his printing partner, James Parker, in 1751, and in his Albany Plan of Union of 1754.

After his death, Canassatego became an English literary figure, the hero of John Shebbeare's *Lydia, or Filial Piety,* published in 1755. With the flowery eloquence prized by romantic novelists of his time, Shebbeare fictionalized Canassatego as superhuman, beyond even the "noble savage" image of Indians that was so popular in Europe. In Shebbeare's book, Canassatego—having saved a helpless English maiden from a predatory ship captain during a voyage across the Atlantic Ocean—became judge and jury for all that was contradictory and corrupt in mid-eighteenth-century England.

Amplified by Benjamin Franklin's talents as author and publisher, the words of the real Canassatego echoed through the years to the eve of the American Revolution. In 1775, at a meeting between colonial representatives and Iroquois leaders near Albany, New York, the colonists told the sachems that, in uniting against England, they were heeding the advice Canassatego had given at Lancaster in 1744.

SEE ALSO:

Albany Plan of Union; Franklin, Benjamin; French and Indian War; Hendrick; Iroquois Confederacy; Onondaga.

CANOES

From Hudson Bay to Tierra del Fuego, the traditional, primary transportation across water for Native people was the canoe and its relatives: the kayak, the umiak, and the bull boat. In its many forms, the canoe has been adapted to many different kinds of travel, including oceans, lakes, and great river complexes. *Canoe* is originally a Carib term, probably indicating oceangoing capability. As a *pirogue,* it is an Arawak word from the central Caribbean, indicating a vessel for inland waters.

For Native people, the canoe has an identity, a personal nature that grows as it is used. This is not some utilitarian craft but a part of the carver as well as the family or hunter who uses the canoe. First of all, the canoe is taken from a tree that is given great respect. As a provider of many gifts, trees such as the birch or the red cedar are honored for all the things for which they can be used. This makes the canoe, with all of its uses, a great expression of this gift.

The cultures of the Atlantic coast of North America had oceangoing vessels that sailed up and down the length of the coast. The inland tribes of the rivers and lakes—the Anishinabe (Ojibwe/Chippewa), among others—used birchbark canoes. The Lakota took their families and belongings across the flooding Platte River in bull boats of buffalo hide stretched over wooden frames. Europeans entering the great river complexes of the Ohio and Mississippi were introduced to the virtues of carved canoes. Finally, cultures of the West Coast—from the Tongva, in what is now southern California, to the Tlingit, in what is now southern Alaska—used variations of the carved oceangoing canoe.

A Cree trapper in his canoe on Lake Bourinot, in northern Quebec, Canada.

The Algonquian trading canoes, such as the *rabeska* (a large fur-trade canoe), were adapted throughout North America. Many traditional people felt that all they needed to survive was such a canoe and a paddle. Today, old birch trees are harder to find than they once were, but canoes are still being made for touring and hunting.

The carved canoes included over a dozen different styles and hundreds of variations, including the ancient "head" canoe of the Tlingit; the sixty-foot (eighteen-meter) northern Haida canoes that carried up to 8 tons (7.28 metric tons) of trade goods on journeys as far south as the Russian River in northern California; the Nootkan double-sail whaling canoes; and the Coast Salish canoes of Puget Sound in Washington state. The carved canoes are the largest works of utilitarian art in the world. They were carved with great care to last hundreds of years and go over extremely rough seas.

When Captain James Cook first visited the Haida and copied their canoe designs, a fresh idea made its way to mercantile England. The sleek, efficient hull design of the Haida's cedar canoes served as the model for the clipper ship, which cut transoceanic travel time drastically and formed the basis of great European trading empires. Deep-ocean whaling, which also once provided much of the underpinning of European prosperity, was based on Native canoe abilities, too.

Canoes had a variety of specialized purposes. Some were used for salmon trolling or halibut gaffing. Some were used to lay out nets or herring weirs (fences), and some to enter kelp beds to catch sea otters or estuaries to set nets for ducks. Some canoes were used for transporting cargo, and some were used for transporting people long distances for purposes of trade or war.

There were canoes specifically designed for the strategies of battle, in which one canoe attempted to ram the other while warriors used the vessels as shields, balancing behind the hull and shooting arrows and spears to stop the ramming. Each kind of canoe had a slightly different shape and balance.

The carvers who hewed a canoe started with a great log in a cedar grove. Large amounts of wood were chopped from the log before a shape began to emerge. The carver worked with great respect, helping his vision take shape as if it already existed within the tree and simply needed to be brought out. Eventually, the shape was refined to achieve the proper hull formation. Then the interior was filled with water and hot rocks in order to spread the sides of the canoe.

In recent times in the Pacific Northwest, it seemed that the great canoes and canoe voyages were only a memory, along with the forests that provided the carvers with logs. Then, the Heiltsuk Nation of British Columbia, Canada, carved the *Glwa* and paddled it to Expo '86 in Vancouver. Bill Reid, a famous Haida carver, also carved the *Lootas* that was paddled to Haida Gwai in the same period.

In the summer of 1989, the Quileute of the Olympic Peninsula in Washington initiated a 350-mile (565.5-kilometer) "Paddle to Seattle." David Forlines carved several canoes as a school project and helped Richard Mike complete an Elwha canoe. They were joined by canoes and paddlers from various coast tribes. The Heiltsuk *Glwa* also came to Seattle, and there Frank Brown issued a challenge to join the Heiltsuk for a *Qatuwas* (great gathering).

Twenty-seven nations pulled canoes into Bella Bella, British Columbia, to be welcomed by the Heiltsuk Nation in the summer of 1994. This was the greatest canoe gathering in history, and the Heiltsuk people received great honor, which they shared with other U.S. and Canadian tribes. The Quileute, Lower Elwha S'Klallam, and Suquamish nations had traveled as far as twelve hundred miles (over nineteen hundred kilometers) to the gathering. At Qatuwas, each tribe presented its dances and songs and feasted other tribes over a period of six days. Since this event, there have been many other programs as part of what is recognized as a cultural resurgence among U.S. and Canadian canoe tribes. For example, there have been two Cedar Tree Conferences to bring various tribes together to plan new cultural forms and to share stories of the canoe. In the summer of 1994, many newly carved canoes converged on Victoria, British Columbia, to open the Commonwealth Games. The great

canoes also came to Elliott Bay in Seattle as part of the Salmon Homecoming and were welcomed by Heiltsuk, Suquamish, and Muckleshoot leaders.

For the canoe tribes of the Pacific Northwest, a great sense of unity has been accomplished. All of the recent voyages and gatherings have demonstrated how a tribe's cultural identity can be recovered. Native people are now writing books and songs about the canoe resurgence, which in turn has helped bring about a revival of related aspects of Native cultures. For example, the weaving of cedar-bark hats and rain capes enables people to wear traditional regalia during ceremonies and canoe welcomes. Masks are being carved, canoe bailers and sails are being woven, and paddles are found in many Native homes.

The Chumash and Tongva peoples also had oceangoing canoes. These were of planked redwood with long pole paddles, and they carried from three to nine paddlers. The technology needed to make such vessels was lost during the disastrous wars and removal policies enacted by the U.S. government against California cultures. Recently, thousands of pages of ethnographic writings have been discovered, containing explicit instructions on how to make and use these canoes, including related songs, ceremonies, and other traditions. Representatives of the Tongva have joined in Northwest Coast cultural activities, and it is hoped that the tribes will join for further journeys and gatherings.

A cultural resurgence implies that nothing was lost but is only waiting for the right time to return. This has been the case with the canoe traditions. The old technologies, songs, and rituals have once again become available. Many people consider this cultural renewal as being in partnership with a renewed environmental awareness, with the rebirth of the canoes tied to the return of salmon and shellfish, the maintenance of rivers, and the replanting of cedar groves.

For the future, each of the canoe tribes is establishing canoe clubs, different from racing clubs, with emphasis on carving, traditions, and family-based events. The Quinault have carved three great canoes. The Hoh and the Quileute are making several new canoes to go with the three they took to Seattle and Bella Bella. The S'Klallam have more than five canoes, making a flotilla that proudly entered Heiltsuk territory. The Suquamish are finishing a great canoe, and the Puyallup and Squaxin Island people are beginning their efforts. In the future, they will be joined by other nations as they involve their young people in these activities. The canoe resurgence has become a powerful alternative to the despair and acculturation that once seemed unavoidable among Native people in North America.

— T. Heidlebaugh

SEE ALSO:

Cook, Captain James; "Paddle to Seattle."

SUGGESTED READINGS:

Lincoln, Leslie. *Coast Salish Canoes*. Seattle: Center for Wooden Boats, 1991.

Gidmark, David. *Birchbark Canoe*. Burnstown, Ontario: General Store Publishing House, 1989.

CANONICUS (c. 1560–1647)

Canonicus of the Narragansetts was one of the earliest Native American leaders to observe the settlements of the English Puritans in New England. He also was a major source of support for Puritan dissident Roger Williams in his struggle to establish an independent colony in what later became Rhode Island.

At their height, the Narragansetts, with Canonicus as one of their leaders, held sway over the area from Narragansett Bay in the east to the Pawcatuck River in the west. The Narragansetts were rarely warlike, but their large numbers (about four thousand men of warrior age in the early seventeenth century) usually prevented other Native nations from attacking them.

When the Pilgrims arrived in New England, Canonicus, in resistance to this foreign encroachment, sent to the Plymouth colony a traditional declaration of war: a bundle of arrows in a rattlesnake skin. Governor William Bradford of Plymouth answered this ultimatum with one of his own: He filled the rattlesnake skin with powder and shot and sent it back to Canonicus. But Canonicus refused to accept it, and thus war was averted.

Roger Williams, a member of the Massachusetts Bay colony, became close to Canonicus as well

as to Canonicus's Wampanoag counterpart, Massasoit. With both, Williams traveled in the forest for days at a time, learning what he could of their languages, societies, and opinions.

When word reached Boston that the Pequots were urging other Indians, including Canonicus's Narragansetts, to drive the Massachusetts Bay settlements into the sea, the Massachusetts Council sent urgent pleas to Williams to use his "utmost and speediest Endeavors" to keep the Narragansetts out of it. Within hours after the appeal arrived in the hands of an Indian runner, "scarce acquainting my wife," Williams boarded "a poor Canow & . . . cut through a stormie Wind and with great seas, euery minute in hazard of life to the Sachim's [Canonicus's] howse." [original spellings retained] After traveling thirty miles (forty-eight kilometers) in the storm, Williams put into port in a Narragansett town larger than most of the colonial settlements of the day, knowing that the success or failure of the Pequot initiative might rest on whether he could dissuade his friends from joining the Pequots in the uprising.

Canonicus listened to Williams with Miantonomo, his son, at his side. The younger sachem (leader) was assuming the duties of leadership piecemeal as his father aged. The three men decided to seal an alliance, and within a few days, officials from Boston were double-timing through the forest to complete the necessary paperwork. Later, Williams also won alliances with the Mohegan and Massachuset nations, swinging the balance of power against the Pequots and their allies.

SEE ALSO:

Massachusetts; Massasoit; Narragansett; Pequot War; Massasoit; Rhode Island; Wampanoag.

CANYON DE CHELLY

Canyon de Chelly is located entirely within the Navajo Nation in northeastern Arizona. The mouth of the canyon is near the town of Chinle. In 1931, the United States made Canyon de Chelly a national monument consisting of 130 square miles (338 square kilometers). It contains hundreds of archaeological sites, some of them spectacular cliff

Chauncey Neboyia and his grandson John Joe Yellowman herding sheep in Canyon de Chelly.

Eighty-year-old Chauncey Neboyia and his wife, Dorothy, two of the last remaining Navajo residents of Canyon de Chelly, are shown holding portraits of themselves from fifty years ago

dwellings. It is also famous for its rock paintings, with some of the best known dating from the Basketmaker culture period before 700 C.E.

The area consists of two adjoining canyons, Canyon del Muerto and Canyon de Chelly. Both are from 500 to 1,000 feet (150 to 300 meters) deep and carved in sandstone. The word *chelly*, pronounced SHAY, is a Spanish corruption of the Navajo word *tsegi*, which means canyon. Navajo families live in the canyons, which are not open to the public unless visitors are accompanied by a guide. The canyons are also dangerous to those not familiar with them because they contain areas of quicksand and are subject to flash flooding.

Humans have inhabited the canyons for more than two thousand years. Basketmaker sites, dating up to about 700 C.E., reveal an early stage of Pueblo cultural development before pottery and the bow and arrow came into use. From 700 to 1300 C.E. is considered the Anasazi period of Pueblo cultural

development. This is when stone masonry apartments and cliff dwellings were constructed. Severe, prolonged drought forced the canyons to be abandoned by the Anasazi around 1300 C.E.

The Hopis used the canyons for seasonal agriculture until the Navajos began expanding into the area around 1700. In 1864, Massacre Cave in Canyon de Chelly was the site of a battle in which 115 Navajos were killed by a detachment of the U.S. Army under the command of Colonel Kit Carson. At that time, eight thousand Navajos were forcibly marched to a concentration camp at Bosque Redondo in eastern New Mexico, where they were held captive for four years before being allowed to return home in 1868.

In 1882, an expedition from the Smithsonian Institution led by James Stevenson gave the area the name by which it is now known. The expedition party was awed by the spectacular beauty of the canyons. Of particular note are the layers of strata in the canyon walls, which change color throughout the day under different light conditions.

Among the more notable cliff dwellings and other sites within the national monument are Antelope House Ruins, Junction Ruins, Mummy Cave, Sliding Rock Ruins, Standing Crow Ruins, and White House Ruins. White House Ruins is the only site that may be visited without a guide. It is reached by a hiking trail leading down from White House Overlook, which is 6 miles (9.7 kilometers) from the monument headquarters on the 22-mile (35.4-kilometer) Rim Drive. The foot path is a 2.5-mile (4-kilometer) round trip that requires climbing down into the canyon and then back up; it also requires wading across Tsegi Creek. The monument contains a visitors center, a campground, and picnic sites, with other accommodations nearby in the town of Chinle.

White House Ruins is the only site in Canyon de Chelly that may be visited without a guide. It is reached by a trail leading down from the Rim Drive.

SEE ALSO:
Anasazi; Basketmaker Culture; Bosque Redondo; Cliff Dwellings.

CAPTAIN JACK (KINTPUASH)
(c. 1840–1873)

In the 1850s, the Euro-American colonizers were just becoming known to the Modocs and began taking their land in northern California. The invaders attempted to exterminate the tribe, and the Modocs retaliated. Kintpuash, otherwise known as Captain Jack, was a young Modoc who believed there could be peace among the settlers. But after befriending the settlers, Kintpuash learned that many could be greedy and hard to get along with.

During the U.S. Civil War, the Modocs, from the Tule Lake region along the Oregon border, were having trouble surviving. Non-Indian settlers wanted them removed from their own country. Politicians arranged for a treaty between the government and the Modocs for removal. Captain Jack and other headmen of the Modocs signed a treaty to move to a reservation in Oregon. The Modocs were placed on the Klamath reservation.

The Klamaths treated the Modocs as intruders, and life was difficult. When he saw that the Modocs were starving, Jack led them off the reservation into the Lost River Valley in search of game and fish. The government ordered the Modocs back to the Klamath reservation in 1872, but Captain Jack refused to go. The cavalry asked Jack to set down his weapons, but shortly after he did, a fight between the soldiers and the Modocs ensued. The Modocs retreated to the California lava beds to hide.

A band of Modocs led by Hooker Jim had killed settlers in a shootout, and the cavalry was now out to stop the Modocs. When the cavalry surrounded the Modocs, Captain Jack called a council to discuss surrendering. They voted to fight.

Captain Jack's people managed to fight off the army on January 17, 1873. None of the Modocs were killed or seriously injured in the fight, and they expected the soldiers to return.

Commissioners, including General Edward R. S. Canby, were sent from Washington to discuss with Jack the possibility of delivering Hooker Jim into the government's hands. In return, the other Modocs would be guaranteed a safe passage.

For many days, Captain Jack and General Canby talked, but Jack refused to surrender his own men to be hanged in Oregon after being tried by white men. Hooker Jim's band forced Captain Jack to promise to kill Canby if he did not submit to Jack's requests. When the general refused the requests—safe passage and a reservation for the Modocs—Captain Jack killed him.

The Modocs retreated to their stronghold in the lava beds and fought the advancing army. Hooker Jim's band chose surrender to the army. He was given protection, and his band set out to find and betray Captain Jack.

The fight went on for several days, with the Modocs hiding in rock crevices and indentions. Jack was finally caught and arrested, along with three of his warriors who had stayed near him to the end.

The men were tried in Oregon in July 1873 with no attorney to represent them and very little understanding of the English language. Hooker Jim and his followers were witnesses against Captain

Jack. On October 3, 1873, Captain Jack was hanged. The following night, his body was taken and embalmed; it later showed up in eastern cities as a carnival attraction for a ten-cent admission.

The survivors of Captain Jack's band were exiled to Indian Territory until 1909 when the government permitted the remaining fifty-one to return to the Klamath reservation in Oregon.

SEE ALSO:
Modoc; Oklahoma.

CARIBBEAN, INDIGENOUS CULTURES OF

The Caribbean Sea is a partially enclosed body of water in the Western Hemisphere bordered by the South American countries of Venezuela and Colombia on the south, Mexico and the Central America countries of Panama, Costa Rica, Nicaragua, Honduras, Guatemala, and Belize on the west, and the islands of the West Indies on the north and east. The West Indies forms the nucleus of the inhabited Caribbean region and consists of two main island groups: the Greater Antilles (Cuba, Jamaica, Hispaniola, and Puerto Rico) to the north and the Lesser Antilles to the east.

Many of these are small volcanic islands, with coral reefs and irregular shorelines. Early inhabitants found six different types of environments throughout the islands: tropical rain forests, dry forests, savannah grasslands, thorny woodlands, cactus scrub, and mangrove swamps. Each type of environment exists because of the amount and frequency of rain in a particular area. Most areas have enough precipitation to provide good or adequate farming conditions.

Until the twentieth century, all the island peoples made their living from agriculture. Warm, moist air masses and the northeasterly trade winds keep temperatures in the comfortable seventy- to eighty-degree F. (twenty- to twenty-seven-degree C.) range year-round, but the tropical disturbances that cause torrential rains on some islands during June, July, and August also produce deadly hurricanes.

At the time of European contact, the Caribbean was home to three major groups of people, all of whom had immigrated from South America. Probably the oldest group was the Ciboney, who lived in small family groups along the northwest coasts of Cuba and Hispaniola. Their economy was based on collecting shellfish and wild fruits, hunting iguana and other reptiles, and catching fish. They are not thought to have cultivated plants. The Ciboney used only chipped and ground stone tools and did not have pottery.

The Caribs

The other two cultures inhabiting the Caribbean islands, the Caribs and a group of Island Arawaks who are known as the Taino, were far more advanced. Both migrated from tropical rain forests north of the Amazon and both brought an advanced agricultural system of root planting they called *conuco*.

The Caribs include people known as the Caniba, Galibi, Garifuna, Karifuna, and Kalinya. Today, they are found mainly in north coastal Honduras, Belize, Dominica, St. Vincent, Trinidad, Venezuela, Guyana, Surinam, French Guiana, and Brazil. The Caribs actually make up a family of many indigenous nations, some of which have lost any Carib language and speak Island Arawak today.

Some Carib groups migrated from the Guyana-Surinam area to the area of Trinidad and the Antilles. There they mixed with Arawaks to produce the later Garifuna people (who now speak an Arawak language). Columbus and his fellow Spanish explorers, who wished to enslave the Caribs for sale in Europe and Africa, portrayed the Caribs as cannibalistic demons. Having characterized the

A Carib boy in Belize.

Caribs in this way, the Europeans attacked and enslaved many indigenous people of the Caribbean and burned the letter "C" onto their faces.

Island and coastal Caribs were excellent navigators. They crossed much of the Caribbean in huge canoes fitted with woven cloth or fiber sails. The canoes carried merchandise as well as people. Where land was fertile (for example, along the lower Amazon, on the Caribbean Islands, and along the coast of Brazil), the Caribs practiced *conuco* (their sophisticated system of raising root plants), which provided them with an abundant supply of starch and sugar. They burned fertile forest areas, formed mounds out of the rich ash, and then planted bitter yucca (cassava), yams, peanuts, and other root plants, as well as peppers, corn, beans, tobacco, and squash. Fishing and hunting supplied a great variety of fish, birds, reptiles, and (where available) sea mammals such as the manatee and other members of the group known as sea cows.

The political organization of the Caribs was unobserved during the period of 1492 to the middle of the 1600s, but the Spanish were quite impressed with the size and quality of houses on Martinique (Matinino) and other islands. They were also impressed with the trade carried on by the people of coastal Venezuela and by their bright cotton scarves and the gold alloy (guanin) that they used.

There are many different Carib nations, each with somewhat different economies. In the past, men may have spent their time hunting, fishing, and practicing military skills, as well as making canoes, drums, gourd rattles, and many utensils. The women supervised the *conuco* system of root farming, prepared food, wove cloth, and made the baskets and pottery. The men lived together in communal houses among some groups, and women lived in separate huts. Other groups lived together in long houses formed around a central plaza, as many still do. Today many Garifuna and other Caribs live in houses like those of the Caribbean region in general. Men enjoyed several kinds of fermented drinks and some smoked tobacco. They also had plenty of time for feasts and dances and for soccerlike ball games.

Experts in building and managing boats, the men were also warriors who were forced after 1492 to constantly defend their islands and coasts from European slave raiders and invaders. Caribs also joined Tainos in the defense of Puerto Rico against the Spaniards, but eventually some islands had to be abandoned.

Virtually all present-day scholars disagree with the image the Spaniards painted of Caribs as cannibals. Some scholars believe that Caribs occasionally practiced cannibalism as part of religious rites (in which they supposedly tortured, killed, and then ate the bravest warriors that they had taken in battle), but this is denied by others who require

that evidence be examined more carefully. In fact, before the French and British tried to drive the Caribs out of the islands in the 1630s, the Caribs were initially friendly to outsiders and even provided food and warnings about hurricanes to the settlers. They turned hostile only after the Europeans attacked them. In Surinam, the coastal Caribs generally assisted the Dutch, even in the capture of other Native slaves to be sold to the plantations.

After a long struggle for survival, the Garifuna Caribs of St. Vincent were transported by the British to Roatan Island off Honduras, from which the Garifunas gradually migrated along the north coast of Central America. The Garifunas have a vibrant culture in cities such as Dangriga (Stann Creek) and have also migrated to the United States (to the Los Angeles area especially).

Other Garifunas have a reservation on the island of Dominica, while numerous people who are part Carib survive on Trinidad (especially at Anica), on St. Vincent, on Martinique and Guadeloupe, and on other islands by migration. On Tobago, the Carib communities of the late eighteenth century have merged completely into the African-American population.

In mainland South America, some Caribs today attend universities and participate in government politics, while other groups still continue a very traditional way of life.

The Arawaks and Tainos

The Arawaks are a group of culturally diverse peoples who reside in Colombia, Venezuela, Guyana, French Guiana, Surinam, Bolivia, and Peru, as well as on several Caribbean islands such as Cuba and Puerto Rico. Before the time of Columbus, Arawakan nations lived from Florida to Paraguay and from the Andes Mountains to the Atlantic. In spite of the genocide practiced against them by European colonizers, many Arawak groups still speak their language and preserve a sense of nationhood.

Before the Spanish conquest, it is believed that Arawakan groups migrated north to the Caribbean and settled on the islands of the Bahamas, the Greater Antilles, Cuba, Haiti, Jamaica, Boringuen (Puerto Rico), and Trinidad. This group, which are known as the Taino, established a highly developed and politically organized culture based on agriculture, fishing, trade, and the hunting of sea mammals.

A Carib fisherman at Blackbird Caye in Belize.

Where land was fertile, along the lower Amazon, on some of the larger Caribbean islands, and along the coast of Brazil, both mainland and island Arawakan communities were large (often two thousand people or more) and consisted of multifamily households holding as many as fifty people each. They practiced the same sophisticated system of raising root plants, *conuco*, that was practiced by the Caribs and which produced the same crops. For protein, Arawakans, like the Caribs, caught iguana, pigeons, parrots, snakes, worms, spiders, shellfish, fish, crabs, turtles, and (where available) sea mammals such as the manatee.

Because of the warm climate, the Arawaks did not have to build elaborate housing, but they did construct very large ceremonial dwellings. Food was so abundant and easy to harvest that they had the leisure time to design and make superbly crafted pottery, baskets, woven cotton cloth, and elaborate stone sculptures. Both men and women painted their bodies and ornamented them with jewelry of gold, stone, bone, and shell. The Arawaks fermented alcoholic drinks and smoked cigars, as Cubans still do. They also enjoyed ball games, informal feasts, dances, and elaborate religious ceremonies.

Arawaks have been described as a peaceful, gentle, and friendly people, but many groups were able to defend themselves quite well and some were said to be warlike. Villages were governed by headmen chosen from the leaders of the multifamily households. Little is known of Taino politics in detail, but we do know that present-day Haiti was divided into several "kingdoms," each with its own sophisticated government. One of the famous leaders was Queen Aracoano, who resisted the Spanish after Europeans had murdered her husband. Arawak peoples were and are very religious people, with the widespread term *Zemi* used to describe spirits and with priests to help the people on the larger islands.

The presence of the Spanish from 1492 onward had a devastating effect on island and coastal Arawakan cultures. Many people who were not killed outright died as Spanish slaves or from the epidemic diseases the Spanish brought with them from Europe. Many Tainos survived on the island of Cuba, where land was reserved for them into the early twentieth century. Other Tainos survived on Puerto Rico and today are reviving their heritage and identity. But their advanced agricultural practices, large villages, most of their political and social structure, their mounds and temples, and even much of their intricate design work have disappeared. Today, many Arawakans still hunt, fish, and prac-

This Carib woman is a cook at Blackbird Caye in Belize.

tice a sort of slash-and-burn farming. They live in small communities of between one hundred and two hundred people.

Other Arawakan groups, such as the Lokono of Surinam, are integrated into the local economy, and some are even living in Amsterdam and elsewhere in the Netherlands. Millions of Boricuas (Puerto Ricans) of Taino race (in whole or in part) now live in New York, Philadelphia, and other U.S. mainland cities.

— P. Press

SUGGESTED READINGS:

Basso, Ellen B., editor. *Carib-speaking Indians: Culture, Society, and Language.* Tucson: University of Arizona Press, 1977.

Claypole, William. *Caribbean Story.* Port of Spain, Trinidad and Tobago: Longman Caribbean, 1981.

Floyd, Troy S. *The Columbus Dynasty in the Caribbean, 1492–1526.* Albuquerque: University of New Mexico Press, 1973.

CARLETON, JAMES HENRY
(1814–1873)

James Henry Carleton was born in Lebec, Maine. His military career was the most important aspect of his life. His first service was with the Maine State Militia at the age of twenty-four. Later, he received a commission in the regular U.S. Army and fought in the Mexican War (1846–1848).

Most of Carleton's career was spent fighting Indians. He is best known for his campaigns against the Indians of the Southwest during the U.S. Civil War (1861–1865). Carleton commanded the California Column, a Union detachment that entered New Mexico Territory (present-day Arizona and New Mexico) from the west and secured the area for the Union in 1862. Carleton then assumed command of the Department of New Mexico. Zealous, overpowering, and autocratic, Carleton instituted a policy of Indian extermination. He issued orders that all Indian men were to be killed and all Indian women and children taken prisoner as the only alternative to complete surrender.

Teaming up with his old friend Kit Carson, Carleton first subdued the Mescalero Apache of south-central New Mexico, using an aggressive method of guerrilla warfare. His field commanders were not allowed to make peace with the Mescaleros, even if the Mescaleros requested it. Instead, they were to kill any Mescalero who did not surrender to Fort Sumner.

After three months, the Mescaleros were no longer a military threat, and Carleton directed his forces against the Navajos. Under Carleton's leadership, Carson carried out the campaign that resulted in the Long Walk: the journey that the beaten, starving Navajos made to Fort Sumner in order to preserve their lives. The mingling of traditional enemies, the Mescaleros and Navajos, at a concentration camp whose resources were inadequate to support them proved to be a disastrous policy.

By 1863, Carleton had turned his attention to Arizona, where discoveries of gold and other minerals led him to enthusiastically support mining operations with cavalry. His plan was to arm the local citizenry, miners, and "friendly" Indians in order to conduct an all-out campaign against the Apaches. He even called upon the governors in northern Mexico to aid him. This campaign proved to be a failure, serving only to anger the Apaches, who stepped up their resistance to white encroachments on their land.

Carleton continued to serve in the military until his death from pneumonia in 1873. Described by those who knew him as a thoroughly unlikable man, he brought a combination of energy, ruthlessness, and effective campaign tactics to the southwestern Indian wars.

SEE ALSO:

Apache; Arizona; Carson, Kit; Long Walk, Navajo; Navajo; New Mexico.

CARLISLE INDIAN SCHOOL

Richard Henry Pratt (1840–1924) founded the Carlisle Indian School in 1879. Pratt promoted education as a way to assimilate Indians and dissolve the tribal bonds that kept them on reservations. His motto—"Kill the Indian, save the man"—coined during the 1870s, expressed

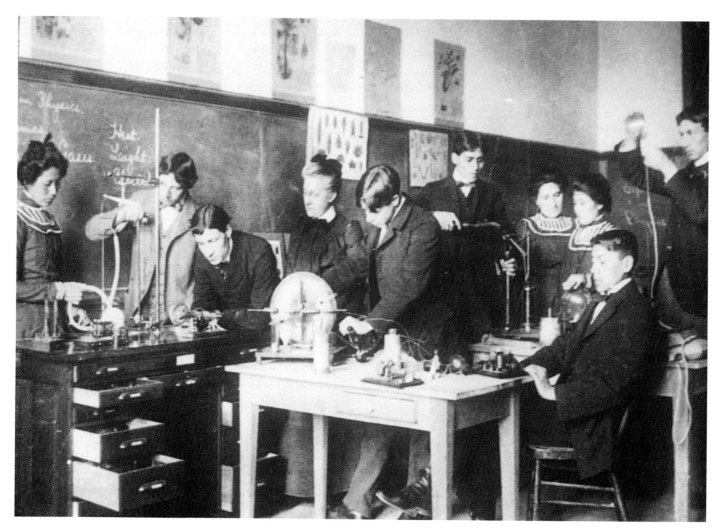

Children conducting physics experiments at Carlisle Indian School in 1915.

non-Indian "reform" ideas prevalent in the late nineteenth century.

Pratt's educational experiment began in the 1870s with seventy-two Native men, most of them Cheyenne, who were imprisoned in an old Spanish fort at St. Augustine, Florida. In 1878, this "class" "graduated," and Pratt approached Congress for funds to begin an Indian industrial school on an abandoned army post at Carlisle, Pennsylvania.

To recruit students for his new school, Pratt visited the Sioux of the high plains. One hundred and sixty-nine students traveled eastward in 1879 to form Carlisle's first class. Included was Luther Standing Bear, who later became a well-known author. Standing Bear recalled his days at Carlisle in *My Indian Boyhood*.

The Carlisle School was run on a U.S. Army model. Students were strictly regimented and forced

to give up all vestiges of Indian identity. They wore uniforms, their hair was cut, and they were forbidden to speak Native languages. Missionaries also were brought in to teach them Christianity. Many students died of disease or other causes, and runaways were punished severely. This system alienated a number of Native young people. It also produced some notable success stories, such as those of author Charles Eastman and athlete Jim Thorpe.

By the turn of the century, this type of assimilation had become national government policy. Carlisle formed the prototype for twenty-five Indian industrial schools in thirteen states, most of which closed after enactment of reform legislation under Franklin Delano Roosevelt in the 1930s.

Pratt wrote a book, *Battlefield and Classroom: Four Decades with the American Indian, 1867–1904*, which was published posthumously in 1964.

SEE ALSO:
Boarding Schools; Eastman, Charles A.; Standing Bear, Luther; Thorpe, Jim.

CARSON, KIT (1809–1868)

Christopher Houston Carson, known as "Kit," was born December 24, 1809, in Madison County, Kentucky. His family moved to Missouri when he was a year old. In 1826, he traveled the Santa Fe Trail to Santa Fe, New Mexico, and then to Taos, where he established his home in Mexican territory. He traveled widely, gained a reputation as a guide, and became well known in the West after guiding several expeditions for John C. Frémont in the early 1840s.

Carson was a prominent figure in the Mexican-American War (1846–1848), assisting U.S. military forces in California; then he went to New Mexico and guided General Stephen Kearney's troops to California. After the Mexican War, he retired to Taos, where he was appointed U.S. Indian Agent to the Utes in 1853. At the outbreak of the U.S. Civil War, Carson was appointed a colonel and placed in command of the New Mexican volunteers.

Once Confederate forces from Texas had been defeated in New Mexico early in the war, the U.S. Army turned its attention to the Mescalero Apaches and the Navajos. General James H. Carleton devised a plan of total war against these nations; they were to be hunted down by U.S. troops in their homeland. Men were to be shot, and women and children were to be taken prisoner, until all resistance to U.S. authority had ceased and the remaining Indians had surrendered. The captives were then to be marched to a concentration camp called Bosque Redondo on the high plains of east-central New Mexico, on the Pecos River at Fort Sumner. In 1862–1863, the plan was applied to the Mescaleros: Within six months, four hundred Mescalero men, women, and children had been interned at Bosque Redondo, and the other Mescaleros—those who had not been killed—had fled to the White Mountains in Arizona or into Mexico.

General Carleton then ordered Colonel Carson to wage a "scorched earth" campaign throughout the Navajo homeland, burning hogans and crops, chopping down orchards, and killing or confiscating Navajo livestock. The general intended to starve the Navajos into submission. Augmenting Carson's troops were Indians eager to acquire Navajo sheep and horses. Indians and civilians were encouraged to raid the Navajos at will. Raiding parties of Utes, Pueblos, and Hopis, as well as Anglo-American and Hispanic-American civilians, plundered the Navajo livestock more effectively than the army.

Carson destroyed immense amounts of crops, camping once for seven days and spending the whole time destroying fields of corn and wheat. Army horses were fed on 75,000 pounds (33,750 kilograms) of Navajo wheat acquired in one raid. The army chopped down an estimated five thousand peach trees in Canyon de Chelly alone. As winter approached, the Navajos began to starve. They began surrendering, and by the autumn of 1864, more than eight thousand Navajos had been marched nearly four hundred miles across the territory to internment at Bosque Redondo, a grueling trek that Navajos call "the Long Walk." They were held prisoner there for four years.

Carson was placed briefly in charge of Bosque Redondo, but he was soon sent to wage war against the Plains Indians. After being promoted to the brevet rank (an increase in rank with no increase in pay) of brigadier general, he retired. He died May 15, 1868, of a heart aneurysm at Fort Lyons, Colorado. In 1869, his body was disinterred and reburied in the cemetery at Taos, New Mexico. Today, a large national forest in New Mexico bears his name.

SEE ALSO:
Bosque Redondo; Long Walk, Navajo.

CASA GRANDE SITE

Casa Grande Ruins is a national monument thirty miles (forty-eight kilometers) south of Phoenix, Arizona. The site contains the only remaining Hohokam multistory building, a "great house" called the Casa Grande.

The Casa Grande was built in about the year 1300, during the height of the Hohokam tradition, but it had been abandoned by 1450. Its durability has been a matter of great intrigue. Most ruins more than five hundred years old are constructed of stone

In 1932, a steel awning was erected over the Casa Grande to protect it from the elements.

and ordinarily have some protection from the elements, such as an overhanging cliff. But the Casa Grande is constructed of adobe and stands exposed to the elements on the open desert.

Measuring 60 by 40 feet (18 by 12 meters) at its base, the Casa Grande is four stories tall. Its foundation was sunk 30 inches (76 centimeters) into the ground. Its walls are nearly 5 feet (152 centimeters) thick at the base, tapering to 2 feet (61 centimeters) thick at the top.

The walls are constructed of caliche, an adobe made from a lime-rich clay found in the desert subsoil. More than 200 tons (182 metric tons) of caliche were used in the construction, more than 1,500 cubic yards (1,140 cubic meters).

The first floor of the Casa Grande is 7 feet (213 centimeters) tall. It contains no doors or windows and is completely filled with dirt, making it, in

essence, an artificial rectangular mound. Three stories were built upon this elevated base. Entrance was gained by ladders to the second story. The second and third stories are divided into eleven rooms, while the fourth story consists of a single room. Aside from providing a commanding view of the surrounding desert, the top story is known to have been used as a celestial observatory. Windows there align precisely with sunset at the equinoxes.

Casa Grande's construction required more than six hundred roof beams. Wood used in the structure includes ponderosa pine, white fir, juniper, and mesquite, some of which had to be transported from mountain regions at least fifty miles (eighty kilometers) away.

The Casa Grande first entered European historical records in November 1694, when Eusebio Kino, guided by Sobaipuri Indians, paused to

Casa Grande National Monument, Arizona.

describe the building and its surroundings. By 1880, a Southern Pacific Railroad station only twenty miles (thirty-two kilometers) away greatly increased both visiting and destructive souvenir hunting. Interest in the site increased after it was visited by the 1887–1888 Henenway Southwestern Archaeological Expedition.

In 1892, the Casa Grande site, consisting of 480 acres (192 hectares), was set aside for preservation. In 1903, the first roof over the building was constructed, and the site became a national monument in 1918. In 1932, a large steel awning roof was erected over the Casa Grande, which still protects the structure today. The monument now features a desert botanical garden and a museum displaying Hohokam artifacts.

SEE ALSO:
Hohokam.

CATHOLIC CHURCH IN THE SPANISH EMPIRE

The motivations of early Spanish explorers in the Americas are often summarized in these three words: *God, gold,* and *glory.* The religious motivation to explore the so-called New World and to convert its inhabitants was one of the strongest motivations of the Spanish conquest of the Americas. Upon landing, Columbus and other explorers hired by Spain claimed the land for their God as well as for the Spanish monarchy.

The Catholic Church was very important in settling disputes that arose during the conquest of the Americas. When Spain and Portugal threatened to go to war over their claims, the pope stepped in and, in 1494, drew a line dividing the claims. Today, this line is the chief reason why most people in Brazil speak Portuguese and most people in the rest of Latin America speak Spanish. The Catholic Church is still very influential in the Americas. Catholicism is the predominant religion in Latin America, in the Canadian province of Quebec, and in sections of the United States, such as Louisiana.

Although the Catholic Church was one of the major agents of conquest in the Americas, some Catholic priests protested the brutality of the Span-

ish explorers. Bartolomé de las Casas (1474–1566), a soldier who became a priest, was among the most critical of Columbus and the conquistadores. However, he still fully condoned the European takeover of the Americas and praised Columbus's navigational skills in crossing the Atlantic so that Europeans could colonize other lands and peoples.

Las Casas wrote books that were filled with graphic detail of the horrors of the Spanish conquest. Inspired by Las Casas's writings, a debate raged within the Catholic Church early in the sixteenth century as to whether Indians should be regarded as human beings or as brute animals. The pope decreed that Indians were human and should not be mistreated. The papal order, however, did not show respect for Indian belief systems. In the same order that affirmed the Indians' humanity, the Catholic Church took charge of the Indians' souls; the order stated that the Indians could be converted, by force if necessary, to the church's doctrines.

Las Casas's writings comprise a journal of the brutality of conquest. "The Spanish found pleasure in inventing all kinds of odd cruelties, the more cruel the better, with which to spill human blood," he wrote. Las Casas described how Spanish soldiers "built a long gibbet, low enough for the toes to touch the ground and prevent strangling, and hanged thirteen [Indians] at a time in honour of Christ Our Savior and the twelve Apostles." With their victims hanging helplessly, the Spaniards tested their strength and their blades against the Indians, "ripping chests open with one blow and exposing entrails." Then, they wrapped straw around the Indians' torn bodies and burned them alive.

Las Casas summoned the offices of the Catholic Church against a practice called "dogging," the hunting and maiming of Native people by canines specifically trained to relish the taste of human flesh. According to historian David E. Stannard, some of the dogs were kept as pets by the conquistadores. For example, Vasco Núñez de Balboa's favorite was named Leoncico, or "Little Lion," a cross between a greyhound and a mastiff. On one occasion, Balboa ordered forty Indians "dogged" at once. "Just as the Spanish soldiers seem to have particularly enjoyed testing the sharpness of their yard- (0.9-meter-) long blades on the bodies of Indian children, so their dogs seemed to find the soft bodies of infants especially tasty," wrote Stannard.

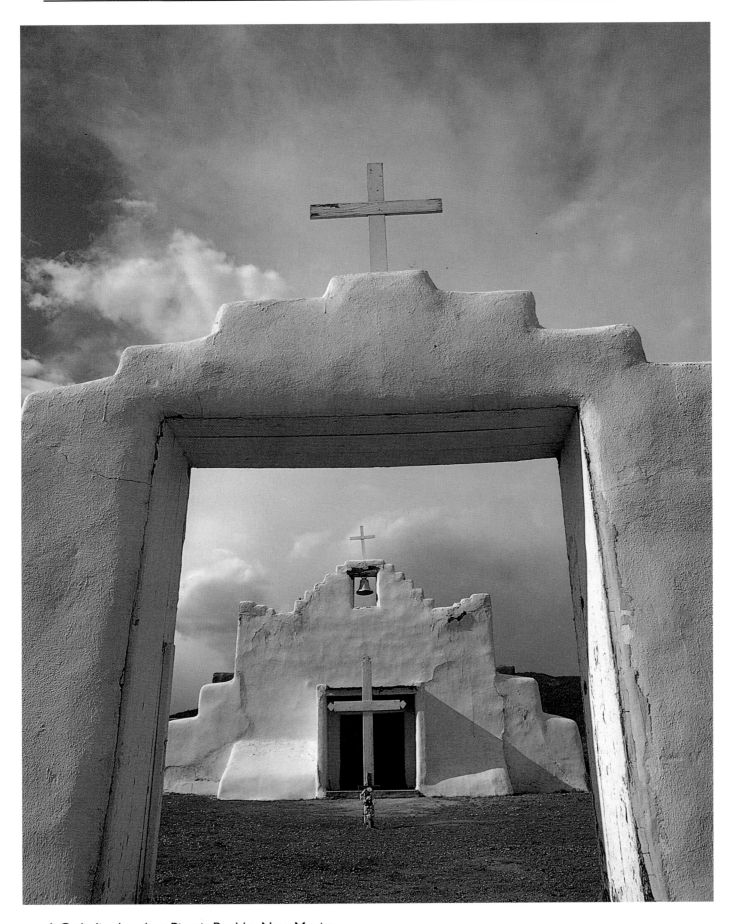

A Catholic church at Picuris Pueblo, New Mexico.

A Catholic church at Zuni Pueblo, New Mexico.

Indians, "not like beasts, for that would have been tolerable, but look[ed] upon them as if they had been but the dung and filth of the earth."

California Indians were not able to mount much organized resistance to the Spanish mission system, which not only forced the teachings of the Catholic Church on Native people but also coerced them to live on the missions and live a life in service to the church and its regulations. Despite their lack of organized resistance to the missions, the Indians did not go into forced labor for the Catholic Church with enthusiasm. So testified numerous friars, who used Indian labor to cultivate bountiful crops and create a rich variety of salable crafts. In the San Francisco Bay area, Native women sometimes aborted their babies rather than have them grow up on the missions.

The Spanish empire and its mission system in California came to a very sudden end between 1811 and 1825, after three hundred years of virtual slavery for thousands of Indians. During the fifteen years after 1811, most of Spain's colonies in the Americas achieved their independence. Mexico became an independent kingdom in 1821 and a republic in 1824. California, at first a province of Mexico, secularized its wealthiest missions in 1834. In theory, the land that had comprised the missions was to be returned to the Indians who had worked them, giving the Indians a chance for self-sufficiency. Instead, most of the land became part of the private *ranchos* run by wealthy landowners, while most of the Indians were driven away. The mission lands and other property were distributed

Las Casas called down a formal curse on Panfi-lo de Narvaez, the main agent of the bloody terror that killed off most of the Native people from Cuba. One of these Indians, a Taino, was offered baptism as he was about to be burned at the stake. The Indian refused baptism because he thought it might take him to heaven, where he might meet even more Christians. In writing of the Spanish conquest of the Caribbean, Las Casas stated that the Spanish viewed

to California's new upper class, composed of wealthy Spanish settlers. Soon after, between 1846 and 1848, the United States gained control of California and the region we know of today as the Southwest.

— B. E. Johansen

SEE ALSO:
Christian Colonists' Views of Natives; Encomienda; Las Casas, Bartolomé de; Spain.

CENTRAL AMERICA, INDIGENOUS PEOPLES OF

Central America is the narrow isthmus that links North America (at Mexico) with South America (at Colombia). This area is bordered by the Caribbean Sea to the northeast and the Pacific Ocean to the southwest and includes the present-day nations of Belize, Guatemala, El Salvador, Honduras, Nicaragua, Costa Rica, and Panama. This strategic location has helped shape the region's history, culture, and economy. The geography of Central America varies from an eight-hundred-mile (thirteen-hundred-kilometer) chain of towering volcanoes to some of the world's densest jungles. Because the coastal lowlands are hot and humid and are often hit with damaging hurricanes, much of the early population lived in the more temperate highland areas (although these areas also had risks, such as active volcanoes and earthquakes).

Many civilizations rose and fell in Central America before the arrival of the Spaniards in the 1500s. These earlier civilizations consisted of small farming communities scattered throughout the highlands of Central America, where they eventually cultivated maize (corn) and other crops.

A Ketchi Mayan man in the Toledo District, in Belize.

Mayan jewelry vendor at Lake Atitlan, Guatemala.

Mayan culture took thousands of years to evolve. By 5000 B.C.E., the Mayas were settled into fishing communities along the Caribbean and Pacific coasts. By 2000 B.C.E., many moved inland and started farming. They grew maize, beans, squash, tomatoes, and peppers, supplementing their diets with wild fruit and game. By 1200 B.C.E., the Olmecs, another major Mesoamerican culture to the north, started to pass through Mayan regions. The Olmecs had become powerful along the Gulf Coast and dominated trade routes that extended from what is today southern Mexico to Costa Rica. Over time, the two cultures started to interact. Mayan leaders began to imitate Olmec styles of jewelry and pottery and even adopted Olmec religious symbols for their own use.

By 500 B.C.E., the Mayas had improved their farming techniques with sophisticated irrigation systems and were producing much more food. Food surpluses in turn led to a population explosion. After the Mayas adopted the concept of writing from the Zapotecs of southern Mexico, their social structure became more complicated as well. Class and social rank became very important, and a small group of privileged elite took power by controlling agricultural surpluses and trade profits. These ruling nobles issued commands to clear out small villages and replace them with planned communities functioning as religious centers. They built massive ceremonial structures where people could worship Mayan ancestors and gods and pay homage to Mayan nobles. Inscriptions on the stone buildings recount the lives and deeds of Mayan nobles, while the paintings on Mayan pottery record their religious beliefs.

Over time, many of these small villages evolved into separate, independent cultures. Societies in the southern parts of Central America tended to remain small tribes, which farmed (growing tuber plants like yams and sweet potatoes) and hunted and fished for food. Cultures that developed in the northern parts of Central America were larger and more complex. In that area, people organized social and political systems where nobles ruled over commoners (and sometimes slaves). The most notable example of this type of culture was the powerful and advanced Mayas.

By 250 C.E., Mayan rulers had become even more powerful. They commanded that architecture and stone sculpture be built in their honor on an even more monumental scale. At this time, the Mayas were also coming into contact with members of another powerful culture, Nahua-speaking warriors and traders from central Mexico. Although they engaged in many battles, neither culture managed to defeat the other. Instead, many aspects of their cultures merged. As a result, the Mayas adopted some of the northern ideas, as well as their clothing, art, and architectural styles.

Between 500 and 900 C.E., Mayan culture reached its peak, with architecture, art, and writing flourishing in more than one hundred city-states. Each center included pyramids, temples, monasteries, astronomical observatories, ball courts, paved roads, plazas, causeways, reservoirs, and aqueducts. In addition to their magnificent architecture, Mayan art included jade carvings and masks, ceramic figures, colored pottery, wood carvings, cotton and feather clothing, and intricately designed jewelry. They also had hieroglyphic writing, bark-paper books and maps, advanced mathematical and scientific concepts, and a highly accurate calendar. It is estimated that more than two million people may have lived in the Mayan Empire at that time.

As populations rose, the nobles of these independent city-states both intermarried and made war on one another. Unfortunately, this chronic warfare and other factors, such as famine, foreign invasion,

and perhaps disease, all contributed to the collapse of the Mayan Empire by 1000 C.E. Although the Mayas continued to live in both highlands and lowlands, the period of their greatest splendor was over. By the mid-1500s, only a few Mayan trading towns still survived along the Caribbean, especially off the coast of Honduras, where traders filled their dugout canoes with cloth and other goods.

The Yucatán Mayas to the north broke up into tiny states that were easily taken over by the Spanish in 1542. The Highland Mayas of Guatemala

A Mayan taxi at Antiqua, Guatemala.

A young Mayan girl with her baby brother, in Guatemala.

(including the Cakchiquel, Quiche, Pokomam, and Tzutuhil) established fortified cities on hillsides and fought with one another for control of precious local resources such as obsidian. The last of these Mayan kingdoms was taken by the Spanish in 1697.

During the colonial period, Spanish slavers took thousands of Central American Mayas to the mines in other parts of the Spanish empire, where most of them died, depleting the population of the tropical lowlands. Many Mayas were taken to Cuba to be sold and shipped as far away as New York City.

The modern Mayas of Central America live in roughly the same geography as did their ancestors, only now the area has different political boundaries. Some four million or so people in Central America still speak one of the thirty or more Maya languages, and many continue to live in rural areas, still practicing their traditional beliefs and customs.

— P. Press

SEE ALSO:
Culture Areas of North America; Maya; Olmec.

SUGGESTED READINGS:

Bachelis, Faren. *The Central Americans*. New York: Chelsea House Publishers, 1990.
Campbell, Joseph. *Historical Atlas of World Mythology*, vols. 1, 2, and 3. New York: Harper and Row, 1988.

CENTRAL AND SOUTH ANDEAN CULTURE AREAS

The Central Andean culture area extends from northern Peru through western Bolivia and is home to the Quechua-speaking peoples of Peru and Bolivia and the Aymaras of southern Peru and Bolivia. The South Andean culture area, which shares traits with the Central area, is located mainly in northern and central Chile and includes the Araucanian peoples of central Chile and the ancient Atacameños and Diaguitas of northern Chile and northwestern Argentina.

The Central Andean area has many different kinds of terrain and climate, including a long strip of coastal desert broken by rich irrigated valleys, the high peaks and deep fertile valleys of the Andes, and the mountainous edges of the tropical forest to the east.

People usually link this area with the remarkable Inca Empire that came to power in the late fifteenth century, but the history of Andean peoples started long before that point. As early as 1000 B.C.E., people understood irrigation and were practicing intensive farming techniques. Even earlier, they built small towns and ceremonial centers, then more complex cities, temple mounds, and step pyramids. Farming and architecture continued to evolve over the next thousand years during a period anthropologists call the Chavin Era or the era of the feline cultists (because of the many cat-worshiping religious cults, like the Cult of the Jaguar). A chavin was a religious center consisting of a stone temple with massive platforms and buildings, ruled by a priest-king. Aside from these scattered chavins, both coastal and highland regions were dotted with small, more or less independent villages.

During this time, people grew potatoes, squash, gourds, beans, cotton, manioc, and, eventually, maize (corn). (Mexican cultures were cultivating corn over a thousand years before it was introduced into the central Andes region.) Farmers used digging sticks and hoes, but they never developed the plow. They also knew weaving and ancient metalworking techniques and developed a unique style of pottery. The development of the loom in this region preceded similar looms in India. Types of weaving were developed that no one can duplicate today.

Around the year 1 C.E., feline gods started to decline in popularity and the Chavin style of small villages dominated by religious centers disappeared. In its place, a half-dozen regional cultures (such as the Paracas, Nazca, Ai, and Mochica) began to take form and, by 800 C.E., developed flourishing and sophisticated cultures that boasted intricate, mile-long irrigation systems, wide roads, monumental fortresses, terraced stone and adobe houses with underground galleries, highly skilled metalwork, and exquisite weaving and pottery. They may even have had a writing system based on "ideographs" indented in lima beans.

By the mid-fourteenth century, there were many of these small kingdoms scattered throughout the Andes. At that time, a Quechua-speaking people from the Cuzco Valley of the southern Andes, who called their leader the Inca, started conquering their neighbors. The Inca Empire started out as a small kingdom, but it soon grew to be the

An Inca drinking container from sixteenth-century Peru.

toes. They also probably domesticated llamas. Maize grew well in such warm areas, and maize and the beer made from it were luxury foods served by the state on ceremonial occasions. Some of the administrative centers along the roads had food storage facilities that held as much as a million bushels (over 35 million liters) of grains and tubers.

Quechua was the official language of the Incan Empire, but there were also at least twenty other languages still being spoken, including the widely spoken Colla (Aymara) language. In addition to their hieroglyphiclike writing system, they also developed a base-ten numerical system and a recording device called the *quipu* that used knotted strings of different colors to keep an accurate account of the goods in their storehouses, as well as census and manpower figures for various parts of the realm. (The Inca government had a reputation for organizing everything.)

Inca craftsmen have become known for their beautifully designed pottery and precious metal jewelry, as well as an incredible range of woven textiles, from the alpaca and llama blankets to gauze and lace and brocade. They used their richest and most elegant cloth to bury their dead. They had an appreciation of wit and comedy and often decorated their pottery and other items with humorous scenes.

Medicine—surgical, herbal, and magical—was another area in which the Incas were advanced. They learned how to use coca as a narcotic and plants like white potato and quinine for their healing properties. They also fermented a kind of beer (called *chicha*) from corn and fruit.

The state religion centered on the worship of the sun. The Inca emperors were believed to have been descended from the Sun god and were worshiped as divine beings. Religious practices included the consultation of oracles, the offering of sacrifices, religious trances, and public confessions. An annual cycle of religious festivals was regulated by the extremely accurate Inca calendar, as was the agricultural year. In this and other respects, Inca culture strongly resembled certain cultures of Mexico and Mesoamerica, such as the Aztecs and the Mayas.

This prosperous and sophisticated world was disrupted by the Spanish invasion led by Francisco Pizarro in 1532. When he arrived, the Incas allowed him and his contingent of about 150 soldiers to

largest indigenous empire in the Americas. Art, architecture, and farming had already reached a peak before the Incas took over. The only real difference in life before and after the conquest was the government the Incas imposed on the Andean people.

The conquest of other territorial groups was remarkably fast considering the limited means of transportation and communication available to the Incas. They built approximately twelve thousand miles (over nineteen thousand kilometers) of roads but had no wheels and no horses. Instead, they used people and llamas to carry cargo. The Incas also had some advanced ideas about farming. They terraced the steep land to be able to cultivate the hillsides. Then they watered them with complex irrigation systems to create valuable new farmland, where they grew maize (corn), squash, potatoes, gourds, beans, cotton, peanuts, and avocados (crops local inhabitants had been raising since 1000 B.C.E.). They developed about seventy varieties of pota-

enter the regional capital at Cajamarca, where they took the Inca ruler captive and then gradually took over most of the empire. At the time of its demise, the empire governed an estimated twelve million people in what is now Peru and Ecuador, as well as parts of Chile, Bolivia, and Argentina. The Quechua language is still spoken today by millions of people in the Andes region, and many native customs have continued during the centuries of European cultural and political domination, in isolated parts of the Andes as well as in urban centers such as Lima. Today, the largest indigenous population in all of South America lives in this region. Many Quechua- and Aymara-speaking people have migrated to Buenos Aires (Argentina) and other great cities, including those of Spain and the United States.

Other groups within this culture area are the Atacamenos and Diaguita of the Atacama Desert and the Araucanians of the central valley of Chile. The people of the Atacama traditionally shared many cultural features with the central Andeans but because of the scarcity of water did not develop large communities or elaborate political and religious features. The Araucanians farmed the central valley of Chile south to the Chiloe Islands. They lived in small hamlets that sometimes joined together in time of conflict. The southern Araucanians, especially the Huilliche and Mapuche, resisted the Spanish until the end of the nineteenth century. More than two hundred thousand Araucanians remain today on scattered reservations. About one-third of the genetic ancestry of the average Chilean is indigenous American, but large parts of the population are one-half or more of indigenous American ancestry. The Mapuche in Chile became very politically active during the Allende period (early 1970s), but were crushed after the U.S.-supported military coup.

— P. Press

SEE ALSO:
Inca.

SUGGESTED READINGS:
Cultures of the World (multivolume series). New York: Marshall Cavendish/Benchmark Books.
Jennings, Jesse D. *Ancient South Americans*. San Francisco: W. H. Freeman and Company, 1983.

CEREMONIES, EXPLOITATION OF

During the late 1960s, a renewed interest in the spiritual practices of indigenous people, particularly in North America, resulted in the exploitation of the ceremonies and rituals of specific tribes and nations. This movement, generally referred to as part of the "New Age" movement, has openly taken, without permission, parts of ceremonies and ceremonial instruments from many tribes in North America and sold these ceremonies and ceremonial tools. During the 1980s and continuing in the 1990s, this movement has accelerated into invading sacred sites that have been used for thousands of years by indigenous people of North America.

This exploitation has been justified by taking certain prophecies, primarily from the Hopi and Lakota nations, and using them without regard for the whole understanding of the prophecies. Objections voiced by traditional elders and traditional medicine people—who have consistently stated that the spirituality of their nations is not for sale—have been disregarded by those involved in this exploitation.

Those who practice traditional ceremonies are offended and deeply concerned about people taking ceremonies meant for specific purposes and using them with other ceremonies and rituals. Elders from many Native nations point out that the lack of true understanding involved in conducting ceremonies creates certain spiritual dangers for both the sellers and the consumers.

These practices of exploitation have not been limited to non-Indian people. This movement has created many self-proclaimed Native American "medicine men" and "medicine women" (sometimes referred to as "plastic medicine men" or "instant shamans") who have neither the training nor the right to identify themselves in this way.

These people also sell ceremonies, usually to non-Native people. The primary exploited ceremonies include sweat lodges, vision quests, the Sun Dance, and the sacred pipe. The Lakota Nation has suffered some of the most flagrant abuse of its ceremonies by non-Natives, people claiming to be Natives, and Native people from other tribes.

Ceremonies and rituals are an integral part of traditional Native American spirituality. Those who are familiar with traditional practices generally understand that it takes many years of specific training and involvement with ceremonies before one is given the responsibility of conducting ceremonies.

It is also important to know that not everyone involved in ceremonies will eventually become the person to conduct ceremonies. For example, just because someone attends a Christian church service does not automatically mean that he or she will become a priest or minister. Someone who attends a class or workshop on Western medicine does not automatically become a medical doctor.

Spiritual practices and ceremonies are the basis for the well-being of the people. Using ceremonies to promote oneself and make money is a form of spiritual exploitation that denies Native people the right to protect their cultures.

— E. K. Caldwell

SEE ALSO:
Hopi; New Age Movement; Siouan Nations.

CHACO CANYON

Chaco Canyon is a shallow canyon in northwestern New Mexico, about 15 miles (24 kilometers) long and about 1 mile (1.6 kilometers) wide, on Chaco Wash.

In the eleventh and twelfth centuries, this small canyon was the thriving center of Anasazi culture at the height of its development. The canyon contains eleven large pueblos and more than four hundred other sites, most of them within an area less than 2 miles (3.2 kilometers) wide and 8 miles (12.9 kilometers) long.

The canyon supported an estimated population of five thousand people. Within a 32-square-mile (83-square-kilometer) area, there are more than four thousand sites. Ancient roadbeds radiating from the canyon extend for as much as 100 miles (160 kilometers) in all directions. Like other Anasazi sites, the canyon was abruptly abandoned near the end of the fourteenth century because of severe, prolonged drought.

A kiva at Chetro Ketl, in Chaco Canyon, New Mexico.

A kiva at Pueblo Bonito, in Chaco Canyon, New Mexico.

Today, Chaco Canyon is accorded protection as a national monument. It is located 65 miles (105 kilometers) north of Interstate 40, between the towns of Farmington and Grants, on New Mexico State Highway 57. Access roads to the canyon are unpaved, and flash flooding can make it inaccessible for brief periods.

Among the ruins at Chaco Canyon are Casa Rinconada. Its Great Kiva, a ceremonial structure, is sixty-four feet (about nineteen meters) in diameter. The roof of this large chamber is now gone, but huge base holes in the floor show the size of the posts that were once required to support the roof. Stone masonry seats line the walls along the entire circumference of the chamber, and a passageway beneath it allows entrance at its center in addition to the regular entranceways along the walls.

The most spectacular structure, and one of the most famous in North American antiquity, is Pueblo Bonito. At one time, this pueblo was five stories tall, containing more than eight hundred rooms and thirty-two kivas. Of the eleven major ruins in the canyon, eight can be reached by automobile.

No one knows how this small canyon, in the midst of an arid and inhospitable landscape, could have supported so many people, or why it should have been selected as the hub of the Anasazi civilization. Mystery surrounds nearly every aspect of Chaco Canyon, including where its building materials came from and how they were brought to the canyon. Even its elaborate network of roads is a profound mystery. They radiate from the canyon in precise straight lines, making no attempt to dodge natural obstacles in their path. Only recently have these ancient roadbeds been discovered, as they are no longer easy to recognize on the ground and can be seen in their full geometrical dimensions only from the air.

Even more recently, a precisely designed rock structure on Fajada Butte, within the canyon, was discovered. This structure, which marks the annual extreme positions of the sun by manipulating both light and shadow, has added a new dimension to our appreciation of the skill and sophistication of the people of the canyon.

Some things, however, are known with certainty. Chaco Canyon was only lightly populated until about 900 C.E. At that time, the people of the canyon began the construction of larger, more compact pueblos. The real construction boom began about 1030 C.E. and lasted little more than a century. By that time, the great structures had been built and the canyon had reached the height of its influence as the center of a large, regional economic complex. That century of sustained creation ranks as one of the most noteworthy achievements in the history of the continent.

SEE ALSO:
Anasazi.

CHEROKEE

The Cherokees and their origins have been a subject of interest to Native and non-Native people alike. Oral traditions (stories handed down from generation to generation) tell of the migration of the people now known as the Cherokees from an island in the Atlantic Ocean to the southeastern part of the North American continent. According to these stories, the island sank after the Cherokees left it in their boats.

When Europeans first arrived on the North American continent, the Cherokees lived in the southern Appalachian Mountains of what is now the Southeast United States. Thus the name Cherokee may have developed from a Choctaw word meaning "people of the cave country."

The Cherokees call themselves *Aniyunwiya* (real human beings). Unlike the languages of the other large Native nations in the Southeast (the Choctaws, Chickasaws, and Creeks, whose languages are members of the Muskogean language family), the Cherokee language is a member of the Iroquoian language family. Most of the other tribes who speak Iroquoian languages live farther to the north. Ethnologists speculate that the Cherokees probably migrated from the Northeast to the southeastern portion of the North American continent at some time in the distant past. In the Southeast, the Cherokees adopted cultural traits similar to those of the other large Native nations who became their neighbors.

At the time when Europeans first came into contact with them, the Cherokees made their home

A contemporary Eastern Cherokee woman in traditional dress.

An Eastern Cherokee man practicing the traditional art of making a blow gun.

By the 1700s, the Cherokees had acquired firearms from the Europeans and, in alliance with various European and Native groups, fought against Indian and European nations alike throughout the 1700s. For example, the Cherokees allied themselves with the Chickasaws against the Shawnees and the Muskogees (Creeks). They allied with the English against France during the beginning of the French and Indian War in 1756. But when British soldiers killed and scalped some Cherokee warriors, a war erupted between the Cherokees and the British that would continue until the signing of a treaty in 1761.

By 1776, the Cherokees had given up large tracts of land within their territory. One man, Dragging Canoe, became frustrated over the losses of the Cherokees' hunting grounds and the burning of villages by colonizers, and he led warriors and their families southwest on Chickamauga Creek, where a new settlement was created near Chattanooga, Tennessee.

The Chickamauga, as this group became known, continued to resist the intrusions from white settlements bordering with the Cherokees. After further destruction of Cherokee villages at the hands of European settlers, part of the Cherokees moved into Arkansas and became known as the Arkansas Cherokees or the Western Cherokees. There, they came into conflict with the Osages over hunting grounds in the region.

in the territory now occupied by the states of Tennessee, Georgia, and North and South Carolina. The first Europeans the Cherokees encountered were members of the expeditions of Spanish explorer Hernando de Soto in the 1540s. Throughout the 1600s, other Europeans began treading on Cherokee territory.

Beginning with the signing of the Hopewell Treaty in 1785, the Cherokees entered a period in which they signed twenty-five treaties and agreements with the U.S. government. Eighteen of these treaties required that the Cherokees give over tribal land to the United States. Not all of the contact between Cherokees and whites was antagonistic or rooted in formal treaties, however. Cherokee people began intermarrying with Euro-Americans early in the history of the United States.

Among the mixed-blood leaders of the Cherokees were Charles Hicks, author of the first written law for the Cherokee Nation, and Sequoyah, author of a syllabary, or set of written characters, created to represent the Cherokee language. Within two years of Sequoyah's writing the syllabary, most of the Cherokee Nation could read and write the language. Created in part as a forum for the Cherokee alphabet, the *Cherokee Phoenix* was the first newspaper written by an Indian nation. The *Phoenix* was printed in both English and Cherokee; its first issue was published February 21, 1828.

In 1828, John Ross, who was one-eighth Cherokee, was elected as principal chief of the Cherokees. Around the time of Ross's election, the state of Georgia had begun taking action against Indians in territory Georgia claimed as its own, particularly as gold had been found on Indian land. The state annexed Cherokee coun-

try into state territory, an action that brought Cherokee people under state laws. Chief Ross brought a suit, known as *The Cherokee* v. *Georgia,* to the Supreme Court, but it was dismissed on the grounds that the Cherokees were a "domestic dependent nation" with the United States as its guardian and therefore could not bring suit against one of its constituent states.

As pressure built between the Cherokees and the United States over land rights, pressure also

Stephen Lowery, a Lumbee Cherokee, in powwow regalia.

John Red Bird Moore, a member of the Cherokee Nation, is shown wearing traditional Cherokee regalia at a festival.

ment, and it was further decreed that the nation would have to share land with the Western Cherokees, who had been forced to give up their lands in Arkansas in 1828 and move into Indian Territory, now the state of Oklahoma.

The removal west, known as the Cherokee Trail of Tears, was a forced march that began on May 26, 1838. Allowed to take only what they could easily carry, people were driven off their land at bayonet or gunpoint. If families were out in their fields working, the soldiers would gather their children, thus making sure the parents would follow. Some of the people got away and hid in the mountains. Today, they are the Eastern Cherokees and reside on the Qualla Reservation in North Carolina. Most of the people, however, did not get away, and over the next several weeks, four thousand Cherokee people died on the trek westward.

grew for the removal of Indians from their lands. And with this pressure came a split among the Cherokees over the issue of removal. Chief Ross remained in the region, continuing to fight for the land. Another Cherokee leader, John Ridge, believed resistance was futile, and at his instigation the removal treaty was signed by only twenty-two people on behalf of the entire nation. Cherokee lands in the East were ceded to the U.S. govern-

The Western Cherokees, also known as the Old Settlers, welcomed the Eastern Cherokees who had recently endured the forced removal. The Ross party of Eastern Cherokees suggested that a new constitution encompassing the interests of both groups be submitted for a vote, but the Old Settlers refused, suggesting that the newcomers participate in the next tribal elections. Followers of John Ridge, who were responsible for signing the treaty of New Echota resulting in the removal, agreed with the Old Settlers. The meeting at which this question arose brought out old animosities among many Eastern Cherokees toward the Ridge party for giving up their land. In 1839, John Ridge, along with Major Ridge and Elias Boudinot (also known as Buck Watie), all of whom had been members of the party that negotiated and signed the treaty with the U.S. government, were assassinated at almost the same time in different parts of the country. Friends of these men charged Chief Ross with conspiring to kill them. Elias Boudinot's brother, Stand Watie, was nearly assassinated but escaped because of a warning he had received. Civil war threatened the Cherokee Nation.

A Cherokee convention in July 1839 brought forth an agreement that the Cherokees would be declared "one body politic, under the style and title of the Cherokee Nation." A national convention was held at Tahlequah, Indian Territory, in accordance with this act on September 6, 1839, at which time a constitution was drafted and adopted.

By 1843, there were eighteen public schools in operation within the Cherokee Nation. The National Female Seminary and the National Male Seminary were opened to Cherokee students in 1851. A press was set up, and the nation began

publishing the *Cherokee Advocate* in 1844. A fitting successor to the *Cherokee Phoenix*, which had been shut down by authorities in Georgia in 1834, the *Advocate* was the first newspaper printed in Indian Territory.

The twentieth century ushered in an era of acts and regulations that formally signaled the termination of Indian nations as fully autonomous political groups. And as various allotment acts parceled out Indian lands, the Cherokee Nation again lost territory to the United States and its land was opened for settlement.

In the 1930s, under the Indian Reorganization Act and the Oklahoma Indian Welfare Act, the United Keetoowah Band of Cherokee Indians drafted a constitution and bylaws. The purpose of the Band was to prosecute Cherokee claims against the federal government and to secure the benefits of these claims for the Cherokees. The Keetoowah constitution and bylaws were approved by the Secretary of the Interior in 1940, making the Keetoowahs a band distinct from other groups of Cherokees, such as the Cherokee Nation of Oklahoma. In 1949, President Harry Truman appointed

Joe Byrd (left), principal chief of the Cherokee Nation, shakes hands with some of his constituents in Oklahoma.

Sequoyah, inventor of the Cherokee syllabary.

W. W. Keeler as the Chief of the Cherokee Nation of Oklahoma, and that Cherokee group approved its own new constitution in 1975.

Because of dissension between the Cherokee Nation of Oklahoma and the United Keetoowah Band, in 1994 the Keetoowahs were granted permission by the Bureau of Indian Affairs to relocate into Arkansas. In keeping with its mission to advocate on behalf of Native people in their dealings with government, the band has been granted jurisdiction in Arkansas to help all Indian people in that state.

Today, there are three federally recognized Cherokee governments: the Cherokee Nation of Oklahoma, the United Keetoowah Band of Cherokee Indians in Arkansas, and the Eastern Band of Cherokees in North Carolina. Numerous other Cherokee organizations are spread throughout the United States but have not obtained the recognition of the federal government that would allow them the ability to serve their people.

— S. S. Davis

SEE ALSO:

Boudinot, Elias; Cherokee Alphabet; Cherokee Harmony Ethic; *Cherokee Phoenix*; Dawes Commission; Dragging Canoe; General Allotment Act; Oklahoma; Ridge, John Rollins; Trail of Tears; Watie, Stand.

SUGGESTED READINGS:

Debo, Angie. *And Still the Waters Run*. Princeton: Princeton University Press, 1940.

Debo, Angie. *The History of Indians in the United States*. Norman: University of Oklahoma Press, 1970.

Mankiller, Wilma, and Michael Wallis. *Mankiller: A Chief and Her People, An Autobiography by the Principal Chief of the Cherokee Nation*. New York: St. Martin's Press, 1993.

Woodward, Grace Steele. *The Cherokees*. Norman: University of Oklahoma Press, 1963.

CHEROKEE ALPHABET

Before their forced removal from homelands in the Southeast during the 1830s, the Cherokees had developed prosperous farms, schools, a constitution, and a written language. The language has its own symbols. In 1828, it was used to publish the first Native American newspaper, the *Cherokee Phoenix*. The language was developed by Sequoyah (who lived from around 1773–1843), the only person in human history to create a written language single-handedly.

Son of a Cherokee mother and an English father, Sequoyah believed that the ability to communicate in writing gave the European immigrants great power. Badly injured in a hunting accident, Sequoyah used his enforced leisure to invent a system of writing, although he had no formal education and was not able to write English or any other language. After he invented the Cherokees' written language, Sequoyah also outlined a system of writing for the Choctaws.

At first, Sequoyah tried to invent a symbol for each Cherokee word but found that the number of symbols would be impossibly large. His work took twelve years, during which Sequoyah was often ridiculed by other Cherokees. Finally, he developed a system of eighty-six standard symbols that represent syllables in the Cherokee language. The language invented by Sequoyah (after whom the giant redwoods in California were later named) has no silent letters or ambiguous sounds.

In 1821, the Cherokees' tribal government recognized Sequoyah's work officially, and by the mid-1820s, the written language had been taught in eighteen schools to thousands of people. Many Cherokees learned its system of writing in three or four days. In recognition of his accomplishments, a bust of Sequoyah was placed in the Statuary Hall of the U.S. Capitol.

The Cherokees began a newspaper in 1828, the *Cherokee Phoenix*, and portions of the Bible appeared in Cherokee. (These were not the first excerpts from the Bible to be printed in a Native language; the first edition of the Bible to be printed in British America was in Algonquian.) Stone pipes carved by artisans of the time sometimes showed Cherokees reading books.

Sequoyah's language also traveled with the Cherokee Trail of Tears (1838) and emerged in Cherokee usage again in Oklahoma. During the Trail of Tears, some Cherokees escaped by hiding in the Carolina mountains. The writing system that Sequoyah developed served them in the preservation of historical records, including many herbal remedies that have been used since. While many other Native languages have died, the ability of the Cherokees to communicate in writing has allowed the language to be more easily taught in schools. Today, street signs appear bilingually, in both English and Cherokee, in Tahlequah, Oklahoma, the capital of the Cherokee Nation of Oklahoma. Many contemporary Cherokees continue to speak, and to read and write, the Cherokee language.

SEE ALSO:
Cherokee; *Cherokee Phoenix*; Sequoyah; Trail of Tears.

CHEROKEE HARMONY ETHIC

Traditionally among Cherokees, the highest value is placed on what is sometimes called a "Harmony Ethic." This code of behavior places a great deal of emphasis on eliminating interpersonal conflict, especially face-to-face anger. In this way, it may be compared superficially to the Iroquois code of behavior developed in the Great Law of Peace. The Harmony Ethic traditionally governs the way in which Cherokees treat each other and how they view their relationship with nature. Under the Harmony Ethic, a person is conditioned by social norms to avoid giving offense to others.

In traditional Cherokee society, a good person is supposed to avoid expressing anger or causing others to become angry; a leader earns respect by listening carefully and not expressing his or her views until hearing all sides in a conflict. A third person may intervene to resolve conflicts between two individuals.

Under the Harmony Ethic, if a conflict is not reconciled, the two parties often go about their business, studiously avoiding each other. In the face of conflict, the Harmony Ethic directs both parties to withdraw. If a conflict can be resolved through generosity, a good Cherokee is expected to share his or her belongings to retain a semblance of social well-being. This value is especially evident with respect to the sharing of food; the Cherokee language contains a special word that indicates stinginess with food, as compared to other possessions.

In a setting in which the Harmony Ethic is adhered to, a person who engages in behavior con-

trary to the ethic may at first become the target of gossip and ostracism, or shunning. If verbal methods of social control fail, and if a pattern of anti-social behavior becomes entrenched, the people who are offended by it might hire a conjurer to cause the offending person to become ill. Face-to-face conflict is avoided at all costs.

SEE ALSO:
Cherokee.

CHEROKEE LITERATURE, CONTEMPORARY

Cherokees are distinguishing themselves in many different kinds of contemporary literature. Probably the most versatile and prolific Cherokee author is Robert J. Conley, a member of the United Keetoowah Band of Cherokees. Conley, who lives in Tahlequah, the capital of the Cherokee Nation of Oklahoma, is a former assistant programs manager of the Cherokee Nation of Oklahoma. He began his career as a poet and as an editor of Native American poetry anthologies while teaching at a number of colleges and universities. His career as a teacher included being director of Indian Studies at Eastern Montana College and at Morningside College. His poetry appeared widely in publications such as *Scree, The Blackbird Circle, Blue Cloud Quarterly, Pembroke,* and *Indian Voice Magazine.* His books of poetry include *21 Poems* (Aux Arcs Press) and *Adawosgi, Swimmer Wesley Snell: A Cherokee Memorial* (The Blue Cloud Quarterly Press). He edited and co-edited a number of small press anthologies of Native poetry, and his own poetry appeared in two of the most important early anthologies of contemporary Native literature, *The Remembered Earth: An Anthology of Contemporary Native American Literature,* edited by Geary Hobson (1979), and *Songs from This Earth on Turtle's Back: Contemporary American Indian Poetry,* edited by Joseph Bruchac (1983).

In the mid-1980s, Conley began publishing novels, both traditional Westerns and Western mysteries with Native themes. In his first collection of short stores, *The Witch of Goingsnake and Other Stories* (University of Oklahoma Press, 1988), his story "Yellowbird, an Imaginary Autobiography" won the coveted Spur Award from the Western Writers of America for best Western short story of the year. In 1992, Conley won a second Spur Award for *Nickajack*, for best Western novel. He was then elected to the board of directors of Western Writers of America. He has proven to be a prolific novelist, with about three dozen novels either in print or scheduled for publication. His work has been groundbreaking in that he is the first Native writer to publish traditional Westerns with Native American protagonists. Commercial publishers had resisted this, telling him that the public would not buy such works, until he proved them wrong. He has created two series. One is a Western mystery series (Pocket Books), featuring Sheriff Go-Ahead Rider of the late-nineteenth-century Cherokee Nation in Indian Territory (present-day Oklahoma). The other is the *Real People* series (Bantam Books), which begins with events in the Cherokee oral tradition before European contact, with each book taking the reader a step closer to the present.

Robert Conley has devoted much of his professional life to furthering the careers of other Native writers.

Conley is also a historian, and among his works is a history of the Cherokee people commissioned by the Cherokee Nation of Oklahoma. His historical novel, *Mountain Windsong: A Novel of the Trail of Tears* (University of Oklahoma Press, 1992), is generally regarded as his best contribution to literature. In 1995, with Conley as coauthor of the lyrics, with Linder Clarsen, who also wrote the music, *Mountain Windsong* made its world premier as a musical play at the Cherokee Nation Heritage Center amphitheater in Tahlequah, Oklahoma. The stage production featured Cherokee international opera star Barbara McAlister and many other talented Native artists. During its weeklong debut, it played to enthusiastic audiences and garnered rave reviews. Conley is also very active in helping emerging Native writers begin their careers. He serves on the National Caucus (board of directors) for Wordcraft Circle of Native Writers and Storytellers and has recently helped conduct workshops for Native writers at the University of Oklahoma, Oklahoma City University, Northeastern State University of Oklahoma, and the University of Memphis.

Marilou Awiakta is a Cherokee poet, essayist, and author whose father was employed at the Oak Ridge, Tennessee, nuclear facility. As a child, Awiakta lived within the confines of secrecy imposed on the families of the Oak Ridge community. Those experiences have shaped much of her work. She is a magna cum laude graduate of the University of

Tennessee. Her first book, *Abiding Appalachia: Where Mountain and Atom Meet* (1978), is now in its eighth printing (Iris Press), and her writing has appeared widely in periodicals and anthologies. In 1989, she received the Distinguished Tennessee Writer Award, and in 1991, she received the award for Outstanding Contribution to Appalachian Literature.

Awiakta's poetry and essays have appeared in many periodicals, including *The Greenfield Review, Now & Then, The Tennessee Conservationist, Parabola, Women of Power, Callaloo, Southern Exposure,* and *Ms.* magazine. Her work can also be found in many anthologies, including *A Gathering of Spirit: A Collection by North American Indian Women; The Colour of Resistance: A Contemporary Collection of Writings by Aboriginal Women; Returning the Gift: Poetry and Prose from the First North American Native Writers' Festival; Durable Breath: Contemporary Native American Poetry; Aniyunwiya/Real Human Beings: An Anthology of Contemporary Cherokee Prose; In Search of Our Mother's Gardens;* and *A Southern Appalachian Reader.*

Awiakta is also a distinguished author of works for children, which include *Rising Fawn and the Fire Mystery: A Story of Heritage, Family and Courage, 1833* (1983; Tenth Anniversary Edition, 1993, Iris Press). The U.S. Information Agency chose Awiakta's *Rising Fawn and the Fire Mystery* and *Abiding Appalachia: Where Mountain and Atom Meet* for its 1986 global tour of American writers, for which the theme was "Women in the Contemporary World." Her most recent book, *Selu: Seeking the Corn-Mother's Wisdom* (Fulcrum Publishing, 1993), is a nonfiction work that many colleges and universities have adopted for course study. An audiotape of the book is also available. (Audio Literature, 1995), featuring music by Creek poet-saxophonist Joy Harjo and her band, Poetic Justice. In 1995, the tape was nominated for a Grammy.

Awiakta is very active in encouraging new writers in their work and has served for many years in the Arts-in-Schools program in Memphis, Tennessee. She has conducted poetry workshops in the Women's Prison there, and she serves on the National Advisory Caucus for Wordcraft Circle of Native Writers and Storytellers.

E. K. Caldwell is among the most versatile of Cherokee writers. She is also of Creek and Shawnee ancestry. Her in-depth interviews with prominent Native writers, actors, activists, and others have gained her a wide readership in *News From Indian*

Marilou Awiakta has written for adults and children alike. Some of her work includes musical accompaniment.

Country, the national, independent Native American newspaper published in Hayward, Wisconsin. She is also a syndicated writer for the *New York Times'* Multicultural Syndication service. Her poetry and prose have appeared in a wide range of publications, including *The Raven Chronicles, Ariel, Inkfish, Perpetua,* and *The Bloomsbury Review.*

Caldwell is also a singer and songwriter, and her music is included on Harbinger Northwest's cassette sampler, *Lights.* She is the author and narrator of *When the Animals Danced*, whose international performances by the Pacific Dance Ensemble of Newport, Oregon, include a tour of Japan. Her first children's book, *Bear*, appeared in the *Animal Lore and Legends* series in 1996 (Scholastic Books). Her work can be found in many anthologies, including *Durable Breath: Contemporary Native American Poetry; For She Is the Tree of Life: Grand-mothers Through the Eyes of Women Writers; Returning the Gift: Poetry and Prose from the First North American Native Writers' Festival; The Colour of Resistance: A Contemporary Collection of Writing by Aboriginal Women; Red Earth, Blue Dawn: Contemporary Native American Short Stories;* and *Aniyunwiya/Real Human Beings: An Anthology of Contemporary Cherokee Prose.* Her dedicated efforts in organizing and conducting workshops for new and emerging Native writers won her the 1993 Director's Award from Wordcraft Circle of Native Writers and Storytellers. She now serves on the national advisory caucus for Wordcraft Circle.

Raven Hail, a member of the Cherokee Nation of Oklahoma who now lives in Arizona, is a prolific poet and essayist and is also a singer-songwriter and playwright. She grew up on her mother's Cherokee allotment in Oklahoma and studied at universities in Oklahoma and Texas. Her poetry, stories, and articles on Cherokee culture have appeared in many publications, including the *Cherokee Advocate*, the *Cherokee Nation News, Blue Cloud Quar-*

Raven Hail has led a productive literary life as a poet, essayist, singer, songwriter, and playwright.

terly, Fiction International, Cimmaron Review, Daybreak, Gray Day, Tosan, Quetzal, The Archive, and *Indian Voice.* Her work has been anthologized in *The Clouds Three, This Light, Arizona Women's Voice, The Remembered Earth,* and *Aniyunwiya/Real Human Beings: An Anthology of Contemporary Cherokee Prose.* Her play, *The Raven and the Redbird*, has been widely used in schools from the elementary school level to Indian studies courses in universities. Her songs are featured on a recording titled *The Raven Sings.*

Betty Louise Bell is a Cherokee mixed-blood writer and scholar who grew up in Oklahoma and California and received a Ph.D degree from Ohio State University. Her first novel, *Faces in the Moon,* is a story of three generations of contemporary Cherokee women who react differently to the challenges of assimilation and appropriation of identity in the dominant mainstream culture. Her novel is the ninth volume in the *American Indian Literature and Critical Studies* series of the University of Oklahoma Press. In the spring of 1993, Bell taught the first course in Native American literature to be offered at Harvard University. She has also taught at Ohio State University and at the University of California at Berkeley. She is currently director of Native American Studies and an assistant professor in English, American Culture, and Women's Studies at the University of Michigan. She also serves as vice president of the Association for the Study of American Indian Literatures (ASAIL), which publishes one of the leading scholarly journals in the field of Native literature, *Studies in American Indian Literatures (SAIL)*. Her work has been anthologized in *Aniyunwiya/Real Human Beings*.

Glenn Twist, an Oklahoma Cherokee elder, won the annual Louis Littlecoon Oliver Memorial Prose Award in the First Book Award competition by the Native Writers' Circle of the Americas only a few weeks before his death in 1995. Twist's award-winning manuscript, *Boston Mountain Tales*, is scheduled for posthumous publication by Greenfield Review Press, Greenfield Center, New York. The manuscript is a collection of short stories relating life in the Boston Mountains of eastern Oklahoma for the generation of Cherokees who were elders when Twist was a youngster. He grew up listening to those stories, told by older relatives and other Cherokees in the community. Twist was an active member of Wordcraft Circle of Native Writers and Storytellers who shared his wisdom and was an inspiration to writers from all the tribes of Oklahoma who participated in the Wordcraft Circle workshops at Oklahoma City University.

Twist's busy and active life was filled with many noteworthy accomplishments. As an aviator in World War II, he invented a system of star-based navigation for pilots that was featured in military publications during the war. He also served in the Oklahoma state legislature. His work has appeared in *Moccasin Telegraph* and is anthologized in *Aniyunwiya/Real Human Beings: An Anthology of Contemporary Cherokee Prose*.

Geary Hobson (Cherokee-Quapaw and Chickasaw) is the former director of Native American studies at the University of New Mexico and is currently an associate professor of English at the University of Oklahoma. In 1979, he edited one of the most important anthologies of Native writing, *The Remembered Earth: An Anthology of Contemporary Native American Literature* (Red Earth Press; reprinted in 1980 by, and currently available from, the University of New Mexico Press). He has also served on the advisory board for the *Native Press Research Journal*, published by the American Native Press Archives at the University of Arkansas at Little Rock. Hobson is also a poet, novelist, essayist, and reviewer. He is the author of a book of poetry, *Deer Hunting & Other Poems* (Point Riders Press), and a volume of essays, *The Rise of the White Shaman and Other Essays*, and has completed a novel that is forthcoming.

Hobson's work has been anthologized in *Aniyunwiya/ Real Human Beings: An Anthology of Contemporary Cherokee Prose*. Between 1988 and 1992, he served on the planning committee as project historian for an historic gathering in July of 1992 of nearly four hundred Native literary writers from throughout the upper Western Hemisphere, called Returning the Gift: A Festival of North American Native Writers. He contributed an essay regarding the history of the festival in the anthology that resulted from it, *Returning the Gift: Poetry and Prose from the First North American Native Writers' Festival*. His wife, Comanche educator Barbara Hobson, served as project coordinator for the festival. She is now assistant director of Native American studies at the University of Oklahoma.

Wilma Mankiller is both an author and a strong supporter of Native writers. Her writing has appeared in such publications as *Southern Exposure* and *Native Peoples* magazine and is anthologized in *Reinventing the Enemy's Language*. Her book, *Mankiller, a Chief and Her People: An Autobiography by the Principal Chief of the Cherokee Nation* (St. Martin's Press, 1993), is the literary work for which she is best known. She has also provided support for Cherokee writers by contributing forewords to some of the most noteworthy efforts of Cherokee authors, including Robert J. Conley's *The Witch of Goingsnake and Other Stories* and Awiakta's *Selu: Seeking the Corn-Mother's Wisdom*. Mankiller is also serving as coeditor of *A Reader's Companion to the History of Women in the U.S.* (Houghton Mifflin Company).

Ralph Salisbury, a poet, novelist, and storyteller, is the son of a traditional Cherokee storyteller. He has presented his work to audiences and over radio and television in the United States, Canada, India, Great Britain, Germany, Denmark, Finland, and Russia. He teaches creative writing at the University of Oregon. He has published five books of poems, four of which are available from Greenfield Review Press: *Going to the Water, Pointing at the Rainbow, Spirit Beast Chant,* and *A White Rainbow.* In 1995, he published a book of short stories, *One Indian and Two Chiefs* (Navajo Community College Press). He is currently at work on four interrelated novels.

Carroll Arnett (also known as Gogisgi) is a prolific poet who was born and reared in Oklahoma. He published ten volumes of poetry between 1965 and 1988: *Then, Not Only That, Like a Wall, Through the Woods, Earlier, Come, Tsalagi, South Line,* and *Engine.* In 1991, a selection of this earlier work, along with new poetry, appeared in his *Night Perimeter: New and Selected Poems, 1958–1990* (Greenfield Review Press). His newest book of poetry appeared in 1995 from Bloody Twin Press. In 1970, after serving in the Marine Corps, Arnett relocated to west-central Michigan, where he now makes his home. His work has been anthologized in *Aniyunwiya/Real Human Beings: An Anthology of Contemporary Cherokee Prose* and in *Returning the Gift.*

Rilla Askew was born in Oklahoma and lived for many years in Tahlequah, capital of the Cherokee Nation of Oklahoma. She presently lives in New York. Her first book, *Strange Business* (Viking,

Wilma Mankiller, then-principal chief of the Cherokee Nation, shown at a White House meeting in 1988.

1992), a collection of short stories, won the Oklahoma Book Award. Her work has been anthologized in *Aniyunwiya/Real Human Beings* and has appeared in many publications, including *Carolina Quarterly, Sonora Review, Nimrod, Iris,* and *Cottonwood.*

Diane Glancy has won more awards than probably any other Cherokee writer. She is both versatile and prolific, writing poetry, stories, nonfiction, and plays. In 1990, her nonfiction manuscript, *Claiming Breath,* won the inaugural North American Indian Prose Award, sponsored by the University of Nebraska Press and the Native American Studies programs at the University of California at Berke-

Diane Glancy has won many awards for her writing, which includes poetry, short stories, novels, and plays.

Glancy also won the 1995 one-act play competition sponsored by Gary Farmer's *Aboriginal Voices* magazine in Toronto, Ontario, Canada. Her play, *Half-Act*, appeared in 1995 in *Studies in American Indian Literatures (SAIL)*. Glancy has also published several books of poetry, including *Offering* (1988), *Iron Woman* (1990), and *Lone Dog's Win-ter Count* (1991). Her second collection of short fiction, *Firesticks*, was published in 1993 in the American Indian Literature and Critical Studies Series of the University of Oklahoma Press, and her third collection of stories, *Monkey Secret*, is scheduled for publication by TriQuarterly and Northwestern University Press. Her first collection of plays, *War Cries*, will be published by Holy Cow! Press. Glancy received an M.F.A. degree from the University of Iowa and currently teaches Native American literature and creative writing at Macalester College in St. Paul, Minnesota.

Rayna Green is a prolific Cherokee scholar, poet, editor, and essayist who is director of the American Indian Program at the National Museum of American History at the Smithsonian Institution. She is the author of more than forty essays in scholarly journals. Her books include *Women in American Indian Society* (1991) and *American Women: A Contextual Bibliography* (1984). Her creative writing has appeared in many publications and has been anthologized in *Durable Breath: Contemporary Native American Poetry*, *Talking Leaves: Contemporary Native American Short Stories*, and *Aniyunwiya/Real Human Beings: An Anthology of Contemporary Cherokee Prose*. She is perhaps best known, however, for editing a 1984 anthology, *That's What She Said: Contemporary Poetry and Fiction by Native American Women* (Indiana University Press). She received her Ph.D. from Indiana University and has taught at Dartmouth College and the University of Massachusetts.

ley and the University of California at Santa Cruz. The book was published by the University of Nebraska Press in 1993 and then won the American Book Award from the Before Columbus Foundation.

Glancy's manuscript of short stories, *Trigger Dance*, won the Charles Nilon Fiction Award from the University of Colorado and was published in 1990 by Fiction Collective Two. She is a two-time winner of the biannual Best Play Competition of the Five Civilized Tribes Museum in Muskogee, Oklahoma, which, since its inauguration in 1973, has drawn strong competition every two years from the best playwrights among the Choctaws, Chickasaws, Creeks, Cherokees, and Seminoles.

Robert F. Gish, who is of Choctaw-Cherokee heritage, is a member of the Cherokee Nation of Oklahoma. He is the former director of Native American Studies at California Polytechnic University and is currently professor of English and Distinguished Scholar at the University of Northern Iowa. His first collection of short stories, *First Horses* (University of Nevada Press, 1993), is an examination of the multicultural complexities of Albuquerque, New Mexico, in the 1950s at the time Gish was growing up there. Gish's other books include *Songs of My Hunter Heart: A Western Kinship* (1991) and scholarly books in the field of American literature. He is a contributing editor to *The Bloomsbury Review* and serves on the editorial board of the *American Indian Culture and Research Journal*, published by the Indian Studies Center at UCLA.

If space permitted, the work of many other outstanding contemporary Cherokee writers could be profiled. They are making contributions in many areas of creative and scholarly writing. Some of them include Charles Brashear, Gladys Cardiff, Karen Coody Cooper, Catron Grieves, Jean Hager, Cynthia Kasee, Ron Rogers, Gayle Ross, the late Jean Starr and Winn Starr, Eddie Webb, Ron Welburn, and others.

— D. L. Birchfield

In addition to pursuing her literary career, Rayna Green directs the Smithsonian's American Indian Program.

CHEROKEE PHOENIX

The *Cherokee Phoenix* was the first American Indian newspaper. It began publication in 1828 and ended in 1834, shortly before the Georgia militia seized its press. The newspaper was actually bilingual (Cherokee and English) and was a product of the Cherokees' effort to maintain a written language of their own. Sequoyah had invented the Cherokee syllabary (a kind of alphabet), and his language was adopted officially in 1821. Four years later, the Cherokee government authorized fifteen hundred dollars to purchase a press and type fonts, half of which were to be in English and half in the Cherokee language.

The history of the *Cherokee Phoenix* is closely linked with Samuel Worcester. This missionary not only arranged to buy a press but helped supply it with type fonts through his religious contacts in Boston. When the *Cherokee Phoenix* began publishing at New Echota on February 21, 1828, Worcester also was a major editorial force. As an editor and writer for the *Phoenix* ("*and Indian Advocate*" was added to the paper's masthead in 1829), Worcester was joined by Elias Boudinot, a young Cherokee schoolteacher.

The *Cherokee Phoenix* was linked to Cherokee efforts to maintain their language and identity in the early 1800s.

swear loyalty to that state. Worcester was one of two who refused. The case (*Worcester v. Georgia*) went to the Supreme Court, where Chief Justice John Marshall found that Worcester's refusal had been legally correct and that Georgia's bid for control of Cherokee land was incorrect. Seeking to promote removal, President Andrew Jackson ignored the Supreme Court ruling, which could have been an impeachable offense under the U.S. Constitution. The whole dispute was sharpened by the fact that it was a states'-rights issue during the years before the U.S. Civil War. This was a time when states' rights—which would broaden the power of state governments to operate independently of the federal government—became a rallying cry for the South's efforts to break away from the Union.

The *Cherokee Phoenix* continued to publish as pressure for removal grew. Editor Boudinot shared news reports with a hundred other newspapers, but shortages of ink and illness among his printers and editors caused publication to become erratic. Georgia officials made obvious their desire to close the paper. As he fought his court case (and remained in jail into 1833), Worcester contributed a number of essays on the Cherokee language to the four-page weekly newspaper. In January 1833, Worcester was forced to leave the newspaper and to leave all the territory under Georgia's assumed jurisdiction.

The last issue of the newspaper was published May 31, 1834. In 1835, the Georgia Guard confiscated its press.

Even after the harrowing Cherokee Trail of Tears (1838), in which a quarter of the Cherokee people died, they began to reassemble their lives in Oklahoma, including publication of another newspaper, the *Cherokee Advocate*.

At this time, the prosperous Cherokee people also had solid-frame houses, a well-organized tribal government, and a written constitution to go with their written language. But in 1828, gold was discovered in Cherokee country, and Georgia asserted legal title to the area, declaring all tribal laws null and void. Under Georgia law, Cherokees who mined gold on their own land became criminals. By 1829, a full-scale gold rush was under way in Cherokee country. As gold seekers swarmed into tribal lands, the *Cherokee Phoenix*, under Boudinot's editorship, warned against proposals to remove the Cherokees and the other so-called Civilized Tribes (the Chickasaws, Choctaws, Creeks, and Seminoles) westward to land that would later become known as Oklahoma.

As part of Georgia's assertion of control over Cherokee country, all missionaries were ordered to

SEE ALSO:

Boudinot, Elias; Cherokee; Cherokee Alphabet; Trail of Tears; *Worcester v. Georgia*.